W9-BKB-244

· Number 141
Spring 2014

New Directions for Evaluation

Paul R. Brandon
Editor-in-Chief

Organizational Capacity to Do and Use Evaluation

J. Bradley Cousins
Isabelle Bourgeois
Editors

ORGANIZATIONAL CAPACITY TO DO AND USE EVALUATION
J. Bradley Cousins, Isabelle Bourgeois (eds.)
New Directions for Evaluation, no. 141
Paul R. Brandon, Editor-in-Chief

Microfilm copies of issues and articles are available in 16mm and 35mm, as well as microfiche in 105mm, through University Microfilms Inc., 300 North Zeeb Road, Ann Arbor, MI 48106-1346.

New Directions for Evaluation is indexed in Education Research Complete (EBSCO Publishing), ERIC: Education Resources Information Center (CSC), Higher Education Abstracts (Claremont Graduate University), SCOPUS (Elsevier), Social Services Abstracts (ProQuest), Sociological Abstracts (ProQuest), and Worldwide Political Science Abstracts (ProQuest).

NEW DIRECTIONS FOR EVALUATION (ISSN 1097-6736, electronic ISSN 1534-875X) is part of The Jossey-Bass Education Series and is published quarterly by Wiley Subscription Services, Inc., A Wiley Company, at Jossey-Bass, One Montgomery Street, Suite 1200, San Francisco, CA 94104-4594.

SUBSCRIPTIONS for individuals cost $89 for U.S./Canada/Mexico; $113 international. For institutions, $334 U.S.; $374 Canada/Mexico; $408 international. Electronic only: $89 for individuals all regions; $334 for institutions all regions. Print and electronic: $98 for individuals in the U.S., Canada, and Mexico; $122 for individuals for the rest of the world; $387 for institutions in the U.S.; $427 for institutions in Canada and Mexico; $461 for institutions for the rest of the world.

EDITORIAL CORRESPONDENCE should be addressed to the Editor-in-Chief, Paul R. Brandon, University of Hawai'i at Mānoa, 1776 University Avenue, Castle Memorial Hall Rm 118, Honolulu, HI 96822-2463.

www.josseybass.com

Editorial Policy and Procedures

New Directions for Evaluation, a quarterly sourcebook, is an official publication of the American Evaluation Association. The journal publishes works on all aspects of evaluation, with an emphasis on presenting timely and thoughtful reflections on leading-edge issues of evaluation theory, practice, methods, the profession, and the organizational, cultural, and societal context within which evaluation occurs. Each issue of the journal is devoted to a single topic, with contributions solicited, organized, reviewed, and edited by one or more guest editors.

The editor-in-chief is seeking proposals for journal issues from around the globe about topics new to the journal (although topics discussed in the past can be revisited). A diversity of perspectives and creative bridges between evaluation and other disciplines, as well as chapters reporting original empirical research on evaluation, are encouraged. A wide range of topics and substantive domains is appropriate for publication, including evaluative endeavors other than program evaluation; however, the proposed topic must be of interest to a broad evaluation audience. For examples of the types of topics that have been successfully proposed, go to http://www.josseybass.com/WileyCDA/Section/id-155510.html.

Journal issues may take any of several forms. Typically they are presented as a series of related chapters, but they might also be presented as a debate; an account, with critique and commentary, of an exemplary evaluation; a feature-length article followed by brief critical commentaries; or perhaps another form proposed by guest editors.

Submitted proposals must follow the format found via the Association's website at http://www.eval.org/Publications/NDE.asp. Proposals are sent to members of the journal's Editorial Advisory Board and to relevant substantive experts for single-blind peer review. The process may result in acceptance, a recommendation to revise and resubmit, or rejection. The journal does not consider or publish unsolicited single manuscripts.

Before submitting proposals, all parties are asked to contact the editor-in-chief, who is committed to working constructively with potential guest editors to help them develop acceptable proposals. For additional information about the journal, see the "Statement of the Editor-in-Chief" in the Spring 2013 issue (No. 137).

Paul R. Brandon, Editor-in-Chief
University of Hawai'i at Mānoa
College of Education
1776 University Avenue
Castle Memorial Hall, Rm. 118
Honolulu, HI 968222463
e-mail: nde@eval.org

CONTENTS

EDITORS' NOTES

A s the title suggests this volume of *New Directions for Evaluation* (NDE) is focused on understanding organizational capacity for evaluation and implications for evaluation capacity building (ECB). Two prior volumes of NDE have contributed to this general stream of inquiry. One was devoted to ECB published over 10 years ago (Compton, Baizerman, & Stockdill, 2002), another published one year later, targeted "mainstreaming" evaluation (Barnette & Sanders, 2003). Both of these collections comprised conceptual articles or reflective case reports on practice that relied in varying degrees on anecdotal evidence and experience as support for claims and argumentation. They were comprehensive in addressing a range of contexts within which evaluation might be integrated.

But this volume is unique. Although it is divided into three principal chapters, taken as a whole, it represents an independent empirical study of the practice of evaluation. It is a multiple case inquiry into the phenomenon of organizational evaluation capacity across a range of organizations with a common aspiration: an interest in evaluation as a lever for organizational change. The research was conducted as part of a larger funded research project and in collaboration with a sizable team of colleagues all of whom contributed to this volume. In the treatise we take a close look at how organization members (evaluators and decision makers alike) perceive evaluation capacity in their organizations and the factors that influence evaluation capacity building and use of evaluation results and processes for decision making. We then look across organizations for crosscutting themes pertaining to evaluation capacity and ECB. What sets this interrogation of ECB apart is its empirical foundation. Our understanding of how and why organizations embrace evaluation and go about integrating it into their organizational cultures is based on our own original data gathered under an overarching conceptual framework. To our knowledge, this multiple case study is the first of its kind to be reported in NDE.

In 1993, Smith joined earlier calls for increased attention to research on evaluation citing a variety of benefits to the field (e.g., knowledge about

The authors gratefully acknowledge support provided by the Social Science and Humanities Research Council of Canada (grant 410–2005–0303) and to members of the participating case organizations for their willingness to contribute to the research. The analyses and interpretations expressed in this volume do not necessarily represent those of the sponsoring agency or the participating organizations. The authors would also like to acknowledge the input of two senior and respected colleagues who graciously offered their opinion on an important aspect of this volume.

effective practice, bad practice, contextual differences; Smith, 1993). He was motivated to write the article by what he saw as a limited response to repeated calls for greater empiricism in evaluation since the early 1970s. In his words, "In spite of the continued scarcity of empirical studies of evaluation practice, such studies are so crucial to the future development of evaluation theory that yet another call for such studies seems warranted" (Smith, 1993, p. 238). Twenty years later, we are happy to observe increased interest in empirical research on evaluation (e.g., published reviews and integrations of research, establishment of special interest groups in professional societies of research on evaluation, and appearance of awards for research). Research on evaluation is clearly on the rise. This is also true in the general domain of inquiry of ECB.

Some time ago, we completed a survey of research on the integration of evaluation into the organizational culture (Cousins, Goh, Clark, & Lee, 2004). That study drew from three cognate fields of inquiry: organizational learning, evaluation use, and ECB. In our search for original empirical research, we were struck by the preponderance of reflective case narratives, typically reflections on evaluation and capacity building by mostly evaluators (sometimes decision makers or other organization members). We believe the pattern appears to be widespread in research on evaluation (see, e.g., Cousins & Chouinard, 2012).

The reflective narrative provides an excellent mode of understanding evaluation practice. We think of it as empirical because it is based on observed phenomena and, depending on the mastery of the storyteller, is able to capture complexity in vivid and lucid ways. But without explicit attention to methods and data quality assurance, it is not possible to evaluate the rigor of such inquiry. We join with Smith in his assessment of the value of reflection but the continuing need "to focus increased effort on the independent, empirical study of the practice of evaluation" (Smith, 1993, p. 241).

While the present volume is very much aligned with this sentiment it represents a unique contribution in two additional and important ways. First, much of the published work in this domain focuses on the methods and roles of ECB rather than on "evaluation capacity" itself. If there are different views about what to build there will be different views about how to build it (Nielsen, Lemire, & Skov, 2011). We need to know more about the multidimensional nature of evaluation capacity and to use this as a foundation for the design and development of ECB initiatives.

Second, much of the work on ECB focuses on evaluation's supply side (capacity to do evaluation), with relatively light attention to its demand side (capacity to use evaluation). Despite the explicit attention to outcomes of ECB in the excellent integrated model of ECB developed by Labin, Duffy, Meyers, Wandersman, and Lesesne (2012), many of these practices have to do with the organizational capacity to do evaluation. Our conceptual orientation to the problem explicitly integrates the capacity to *do and use* evaluation (Bourgeois & Cousins, 2008, 2013; Cousins et al., 2008).

This volume is set out in three distinct chapters. First, with Swee Goh and Catherine Elliott we lay out the conceptual backdrop for the multiple case study on organizational evaluation capacity. In this chapter, we converse with the current literature on ECB and describe the conceptual framework that guided the multiple case study. We situate this conceptualization among other published works and highlight our focus on not just the capacity to do evaluation but the capacity to use it.

The bulk of the research is reported in Chapter 2 of this volume. Here, we describe the selection of organizations in our sample and detail the methods that we used. We then present organizational case descriptions and summaries of the findings within cases. We present the cases sequentially, each having been carried out and authored by different configurations of members of our research group.

A cross-case analysis is the product of Chapter 3 of this volume. The main focus is a thematic analysis. The themes that we explicate are emergent and generally touch on at least two of the eight organizations on our sample. We summarize each and then move to considerations for ECB practice and implications for ongoing research in the area.

We conclude our opening remarks with a caveat. As mentioned, this multiple case study was part of a larger funded research project. The project began with an initial concept mapping inquiry that informed both this multiple case study and a concurrent large-scale survey of internal evaluators already published (Cousins et al., 2008). It is essential to note that data collection and reporting for the individual case organizations took place in 2007. It is only recently that we have pursued the cross-case thematic analysis with alacrity. Having said that, we acknowledge that the organizations that participated in the study are dynamic entities and that each and every one of them is in a different time and space with regard to organizational capacity for evaluation among many other parameters. It is likely that some have strengthened their capacity to do and use evaluation, while others have moved in the other direction. While it would no doubt be interesting to plot the trajectory of change for the respective organizations and the forces, factors, and circumstances underlying such change, this matter is well beyond the scope of the present study. This issue, we take up more thoroughly in our comments on implications for ongoing research in Chapter 3.

References

Barnette, J. J., & Sanders, J. R. (Eds.). (2003). *New Directions for Evaluation: No. 99. The mainstreaming of evaluation.* San Francisco, CA: Jossey-Bass.

Bourgeois, I., & Cousins, J. B. (2008). Informing evaluation capacity building through profiling organizational capacity for evaluation: An empirical examination of four Canadian Federal Government organizations. *Canadian Journal of Program Evaluation, 23*(3), 127–146.

Bourgeois, I., & Cousins, J. B. (2013). Understanding dimensions of organizational evaluation capacity. *American Journal of Evaluation, 34*(3), 299–319.

Compton, D., Baizerman, M., & Stockdill, S. H. (Eds.). (2002). *New Directions for Evaluation: No. 93. The art, craft and science of evaluation capacity building.* San Francisco, CA: Jossey-Bass.

Cousins, J. B., & Chouinard, J. A. (2012). *Participatory evaluation up close: A review and integration of research-based knowledge.* Charlotte, NC: Information Age Press.

Cousins, J. B., Elliott, C., Amo, C., Bourgeois, I., Chouinard, J. A., Goh, S. C., & Lahey, R. (2008). Organizational capacity to do and use evaluation: Results of a pan-Canadian survey of evaluators. *Canadian Journal of Program Evaluation, 23*(3), 1–35.

Cousins, J. B., Goh, S., Clark, S., & Lee, L. (2004). Integrating evaluative inquiry into the organizational culture: A review and synthesis of the knowledge base. *Canadian Journal of Program Evaluation, 19*(2), 99–141.

Labin, S., Duffy, J. L., Meyers, D. C., Wandersman, A., & Lesesne, C. A. (2012). A research synthesis of the evaluation capacity building literature. *American Journal of Evaluation, 33*, 307–338.

Nielsen, S. B., Lemire, S., & Skov, M. (2011). Measuring evaluation capacity—Results and implications of a Danish study. *American Journal of Evaluation, 32*(3), 324–344.

Smith, N. L. (1993). Improving evaluation theory through the empirical study of evaluation practice. *Evaluation Practice, 14*(3), 237–242.

Research Team Members

Courtney Amo, Manager, Evaluation, Atlantic Canada Opportunities Agency, Moncton, NB.

Tim Aubry, Professor, School of Psychology, University of Ottawa.

Jill Anne Chouinard, Independent Consultant and Part Time Professor, University of Ottawa.

Catherine Elliott, Adjunct Professor, Telfer School of Management, University of Ottawa.

Anna Engman, Senior Program Evaluation Officer, Natural Sciences and Engineering Research Council of Canada, Ottawa, ON.

Swee C. Goh, Professor Emeritus, Telfer School of Management, University of Ottawa.

Keiko Kuji-Shikatani, Education Officer, Student Achievement Division, Ministry of Education and Training, Toronto, ON.

Robert Lahey, President, REL Solutions, Ottawa, ON.

Steve Montague, Partner, Performance Management Network Inc., Ottawa, ON.

Other Contributors

Sarah Birnie, Clinical Psychologist, The Ottawa Hospital, Ottawa, ON.

Sharon Campbell, Research Associate Professor, School of Public Health and Health Systems, University of Waterloo, Waterloo, ON.

Anne Vezina, Former Acting President & Chief Executive Officer, Canadian Cancer Society.

J. Bradley Cousins
Isabelle Bourgeois
Editors

J. BRADLEY COUSINS *is a professor of educational evaluation at the Faculty of Education and Director of the Centre for Research on Educational and Community Services (CRECS), University of Ottawa.*

ISABELLE BOURGEOIS *is a professor of program evaluation at l'École nationale d'administration publique (National School of Public Administration), University of Québec, Gatineau, Québec.*

NEW DIRECTIONS FOR EVALUATION • DOI: 10.1002/ev

1

Framing the Capacity to Do and Use Evaluation

J. Bradley Cousins, Swee C. Goh,
Catherine J. Elliott, Isabelle Bourgeois

Abstract

The construct of organizational evaluation capacity is a concept that is receiving increasing attention in theoretical and research-based literature. It is situated within a stream of inquiry that has come to be known as evaluation capacity building (ECB). This chapter reviews evolving conceptions of ECB and recent research and theory in the area. A conceptualization of organizational capacity for evaluation is explicated. The framework addresses not only the capacity to do but also the capacity to use evaluation. This framework has evolved within our ongoing research program and has also informed other research activities focusing on the integration of evaluation into organizational culture. This chapter concludes with a discussion of implications for ongoing research and practice. © Wiley Periodicals, Inc., and the American Evaluation Association.

Evolving Conceptions of Evaluation Capacity Building

Evaluation capacity building (ECB) has increasingly captured the interest of evaluation theorists, researchers, and practitioners alike since the turn of the millennium. Milstein and Cotton (2000, October) provided a thoughtful framework for consideration by way of framing the theme of *Evaluation*

Note: Parts of this chapter were adapted from a paper presented at the AEA annual meeting in Baltimore in 2007.

NEW DIRECTIONS FOR EVALUATION, no. 141, Spring 2014 © Wiley Periodicals, Inc., and the American Evaluation Association. Published online in Wiley Online Library (wileyonlinelibrary.com) • DOI: 10.1002/ev.20076

2000, the annual meeting of the American Evaluation Association. They differentiated ECB from other kinds of capacity building, such as the ability of individuals, organizations, or communities to achieve broad social or organizational goals. They defined evaluation capacity as "the ability to conduct an effective evaluation (i.e., one that meets accepted standards of the discipline)."

Enhancing in individuals and organizations the *capacity to do* evaluation is an undeniably important concern for evaluation as a professional field. As Milstein and Cotton suggested, there exist at least two important and related streams of inquiry and professional work in evaluation that are very much aligned with this concern: the development and verification of evaluator competencies for professional practice and the design and delivery of pre-service and in-service training in evaluation.

We are aware of two recent research projects identifying through systematic inquiry a set of core competencies for evaluators. The first has emerged from a group of American researchers led by King and Stevahn (King, Stevahn, Ghere, & Minnema, 2001; Stevahn, King, Ghere, & Minnema, 2005a, 2005b) and has resulted in an empirically validated set of "Essential Competencies for Program Evaluators" (ECPE). The competencies are organized under six categories or themes: (a) professional practice, (b) systematic inquiry, (c) situational analysis, (d) project management, (e) reflective practice, and (f) interpersonal competence. Another set of competencies was derived from an independent study commissioned by the Canadian Evaluation Society in support of its evaluation advocacy agenda. Known as the Core Body of Knowledge (CBK) project and undertaken by a group of researchers led by Zorzi (Zorzi, Perrin, McGuire, Long, & Lee, 2002), the project produced a list of 23 general knowledge and skill elements of program evaluation. Each element was categorized into one of the following clusters: ethics; evaluation planning and design; data collection, data analysis, and interpretation; communication and interpersonal skills; and project management.

A second stream of professional activity continues to develop within the global evaluation community, that is, the design and delivery of training opportunities for those aspiring to work in the field (pre-service) and those already engaged in evaluation practice (in-service). Despite some recent evidence to show that evaluation university-level training programs may be on the decline in the United States (Engle & Altschuld, 2003; Engle, Altschuld, & Kim, 2006), in many jurisdictions including North America, Europe, and Australasia, evaluation is taught at the level of (mostly) graduate courses available at universities with potential for specialization in evaluation under related degree designations (e.g., public administration, community psychology, health sciences, and educational administration). In addition, university-based graduate diploma programs (typically one-half master's degree) provide an attractive alternative for many persons seeking advanced training. Such diploma programs are increasingly available in many jurisdictions (Cousins & Aubry, 2006). In Canada, the Consortium of Universities for Evaluation Education (CUEE, www.evaluationeducation.ca) was recently formed; many member universities offer such diplomas.

In addition to formal, university-level, achievement-oriented training and educational opportunities, globally, professional societies and service providers continue to provide pre- and in-service training at workshops, training institutes, short courses, online programs, and the like (e.g., AEA Summer Institute, CES Essential Skills Series, International Development Evaluation Training Program [IPDET], Evaluator's Institute [TEI]). Many of these are supported by a rapidly expanding bank of resource material developed specifically for ECB training (e.g., CES Sourcebook for evaluation methods; Preskill & Russ-Eft's [2005] resource book of ECB activities; UNICEF and IOCE's web-based MY M&E web-based platform[1]).

An important consideration when thinking about ECB is a distinction that we have used previously (Cousins, Goh, Clark, & Lee, 2004; Cousins et al., 2008) between direct and indirect approaches. The aforementioned menu of ECB options, which are by no means exhaustive, fall into the direct category. These are intentional capacity building initiatives that are designed specifically to foster growth in evaluation knowledge and skill (e.g., see the ECB immersion project described in Lawrenz, Thomas, Huffman, and Covington Clarkson [2008]). Indirect ECB experiences arise in activities where participants learn by doing. Examples would be practicum opportunities where participants assume responsibility for direct engagement with technical activities in the systematic inquiry process. Interestingly, whereas direct ECB approaches are exclusively intentional this is not necessarily the case with indirect ECB. Baizerman, Compton, and Stockdill (2002) argued that ECB is always intentional and does not come about in a haphazard random way. Yet there is growing evidence from research on participatory evaluation (Cousins & Chouinard, 2012), for example, that learning benefits accrue to members of the program stakeholder community by virtue of participation in evaluation activities, otherwise known as process use.

While concern with the capacity to do evaluation is alive and well, inquiry into ECB has taken a wider perspective over the past number of years. This view encompasses not only the capacity to do evaluation but also the *capacity to use* it. While this was not necessarily the case with Sanders' (2003) definition of "mainstreaming" evaluation: "the process of making evaluation an integral part of an organization's everyday operation" (p. 3), in an earlier volume of *New Directions for Evaluation*, Compton, Baizerman, and Stockdill (2002) frame ECB not only in terms of the ability to do quality evaluation but also to use it within the organizational context. Specifically, they define the term as

A context-dependent intentional action system of guided processes and practices for bringing about and sustaining a state of affairs in which quality program evaluation and its *appropriate uses* are ordinary and ongoing practices within and/or between one or more organizations/programs/sites. (Stockdill, Baizerman, & Compton, 2002, p. 8, emphasis added)

Similar postures were taken by Labin, Duffy, Meyers, Wandersman, and Lesesne (2012) and Preskill and Boyle (2008), both of whom sought to develop models of ECB.

In their conversation with the literature, Stockdill et al. (2002) identified as a lesson that effective ECB requires broad-based demand. The organizational demand for ECB, of course, is inextricably linked to the demand for evaluation, and its sustainability depends on the extent to which evaluation is used within the organization. As we put it some time ago, "The integration of evaluation into the culture of organizations ... has as much to do with the consequences of evaluation as it does the development of skills and knowledge of evaluation logic and methods" (Cousins et al., 2004, p. 101).

Use and Organizational Evaluation Capacity

Thinking about ECB not just as directed activities to foster high-quality professional practice but also in terms of program, organizational, and even societal consequences inherently makes sense to us. Yet, despite inclusion of use in definitions of ECB and recognition of the importance of use to the development of ECB demand (Stockdill et al., 2002), it is our opinion that evaluation use has been underexplored and underemphasized in theory, research, and practice concerning organizational evaluation capacity. Most work in the area focuses on evaluation's supply side (capacity to do evaluation), and little attention has been paid to its demand side (capacity to use evaluation). For example, the multidisciplinary model of ECB developed by Preskill and Boyle (2008) identifies two principal spheres of interest (evaluation knowledge, skill, and attitudes, and sustainable evaluation practice) with some consideration given to the organizational context in which ECB occurs (e.g., leadership, culture, and communication). The integrated model of ECB developed by Labin et al. (2012) explicitly identifies ECB outcomes and the individual (attitudes, knowledge, and behaviors) and organizational (leadership, practice, and resources) levels. Yet, although this is not exclusively the case, these practices and behaviors can be construed as organizational capacity to do evaluation, as opposed to use it. We argue that evaluation use is an essential element of any conception of evaluation capacity and needs to be addressed as such. We now turn to some justification for this claim.

Utilization and Evaluation Theory

In thinking about research on evaluation, evaluation utilization or use is probably the most heavily studied domain of interest in the field (Henry

& Mark, 2003). Much of this research focused on the identification of instrumental, conceptual, and symbolic (persuasive and legitimatize) uses of evaluation findings and the factors and conditions that foster such use. Recent advances in research and theory about evaluation consequences, such as the burgeoning concept of process use (e.g., Cousins, 2007; Forss, Kruse, Taut, & Tenden, 2006; Patton, 1997, 2008) and considerations of use in the context of broader evaluation influences (e.g., Kirkhart, 2000; Mark & Henry, 2004), have significant implications for any consideration of evaluation theory and practice.

Professional Standards of Practice

The production of good quality program evaluation is central to ECB (Baizerman et al., 2002) and it is imperative that ECB initiatives are guided by professional standards of practice to which professional evaluators subscribe. Such standards openly touch on considerations of use. For example, utility has been an explicit and significant element of the Joint Committee Standards for Educational Evaluation, Program Evaluation Standards since their inception in the early 1980s and appropriate uses of evaluation are integral to the AEA guiding principles. Professional evaluator competencies also embrace the concept of utility (Stevahn et al., 2005a; Zorzi et al., 2002).

Evaluation and Organizational Learning

Conceptual and empirical links between evaluation and organizational learning have long been established (e.g., Cousins & Earl, 1995; Owen & Lambert, 1995; Preskill & Torres, 1999), and evaluation may be reasonably thought of as an organizational learning system (Cousins et al., 2004). The results of a survey of AEA members conducted by Fleischer, Christie, and LaVelle (2008) support this perspective through the establishment of a link between evaluation activities and organizational learning and change outcomes. In our opinion, this thinking is part and parcel of Patton's (2011) conception of developmental evaluation where evaluators work closely with organizational decision makers to navigate complexity and enhance innovation. Evaluation in this systemic context is inextricably linked to organizational uses of systematic inquiry and evidence.

Data Use Leads to Data Valuing

Results of our own research have tentatively shown that the successful use of evaluation data in organizations fosters their valuing by members as a powerful force for organizational and program change (Cousins, Goh, & Clark, 2005). From the perspective of integrating evaluation into organizational culture, "data use leads to data valuing" is a hypothesis worth pursuing. Demand for evaluation is not likely to grow as a result of promotional campaigns. Organizational decision makers need to experience the benefits of evaluation firsthand before they willingly embrace it as leverage for change.

Direct Versus Indirect ECB

As mentioned above, direct ECB is always intentional but indirect ECB is not necessarily so. The central operative construct in indirect ECB is process use. Through direct experience or close proximity to evaluation, nonevaluator stakeholders learn new ways of conceptualizing; they learn to think "evaluatively," as described, for example, in the catalyst-for-change approach to ECB presented by Garcia-Iriarte, Suarez-Balcazar, Taylor-Ritzler, and Luna (2011). There is some evidence to suggest that process use and use of evaluation findings may be correlated (Amo & Cousins, 2012). Regardless, the effectiveness of indirect ECB is integrally related to use considerations, an argument consistent with Carman and Fredericks' (2010) claim that "evaluation capacity builders can help non-profit organizations to maximize the use of evaluation information and help them to better position themselves with external stakeholders" (p. 100).

If we accept as reasonable and justifiable that considerations of consequence ought to be integrated into our conception of ECB then a logical next step would be to conceptually unpack this notion into a framework of evaluation capacity that might ultimately serve evaluation theory, research, and practice. As Nacarrella et al. (2007) and Nielsen, Lemire, and Skov (2011) point out, there has been much focus on the methods and roles of ECB but not much attention to evaluation capacity itself. The development and explication of a framework for organizational evaluation capacity represents the main contribution of this chapter of the present volume. To follow, we explicate what we see as the principal constructs of interest and suggested relations among them. We then turn to some thoughts about how this representation can inform research on organizational evaluation capacity.

Framework for Organizational Evaluation Capacity

The framework presented in this chapter has evolved over a considerable period of time, perhaps commencing with our initial foray into the domain of integrating evaluation into the organizational culture (Cousins et al., 2004). We begin by reviewing some assumptions for the framework and then move to its description and intended use for research.

Assumptions

A basic assumption from which we operate is that ECB knowledge and practice, as would be the case with any evaluation-related domain of inquiry, will benefit from well-developed, credible, research-based evidence. As such we are motivated to contribute to the discourse about ECB through empirical inquiry. We are both cognizant and accepting of a range of choices available to researchers who wish to systematically study complex phenomena in evaluation.

Our approach to empirical inquiry is one that embraces the notion of preordinate conceptual structure as a means of guiding data collection, analysis, and interpretation. Yet we are not "hard-liners" in this respect. We appreciate the essentiality of considerations of context and that it is ultimately counterproductive and limiting to rigidly adhere to a preordinate frame when thinking about and studying complex social phenomena.

For this reason, we offer the conceptual framework to follow as a tentative guide to understanding. We specify constructs and suggested relations among them not as a stab at theoretical explanation, but as a tentative set of boundaries to help focus and direct inquiry. Equally important is a commitment to open-mindedness meaning that the framework ought to be thought of as contestable and challengeable in the face of systematically generated data.

Conceptual Framework

Figure 1.1 presents a visual representation of our conceptual framework. The framework has evolved from a prior integration and analysis of research and collaborative exchange among members of our research group. It unpacks an expanded conception of ECB that embraces as essential the notion of evaluation consequences; the capacity to do and use evaluation. We use as a unit of analysis the organization as much of our prior work has been concerned with the challenge of integrating evaluation into the organizational culture (Cousins et al., 2004) and the conception of evaluation as an organizational learning system (Cousins & Earl, 1995; Owen & Lambert, 1995). We turn now to a description of the constructs and their interrelations.

In thinking about complex phenomena we find it useful to consider the nature of the phenomena, the consequences to which it might lead, and the antecedent conditions, factors, or forces that help to shape or otherwise influence it. Associated questions might be: What is it? What effects might it have? From where does it come? In the present case, our focus is on integrating the capacity to do and use evaluation and, as such, considerations of what evaluation capacity is and what effects it is likely to have are melded together. This is represented in the right-hand side of Figure 1.1, the unit of analysis being the organization. On the left side, we represent antecedent conditions and forces that influence or help to determine evaluation capacity within the organization.

Antecedents of ECB. We capture principal forces and influences on organizational ECB in two constructs: sources of evaluation knowledge skills and abilities (K/S/A) and organizational support structures.

Sources of K/S/A relate in a very direct way to the foregoing discussion of evaluation as a profession, particularly with regard to work on the

Figure 1.1. Conceptual Framework Depicting Organizational Capacity to Do and Use Evaluation

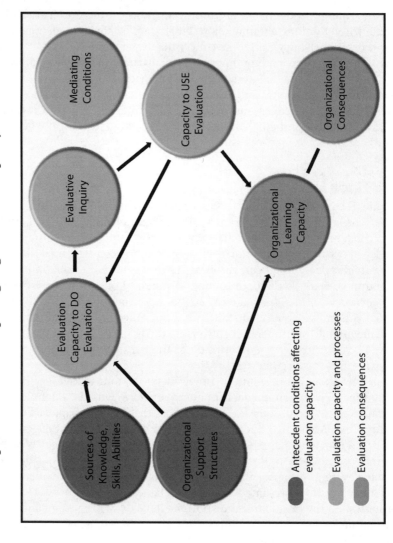

development of evaluators' competencies and most especially to pre- and in-service training. Some conception of evaluators' competencies, whether implicit and informal or explicit and formal (e.g., ECPE, CBK), underlies the provision of pre- and in-service training for evaluators. Training can take the form of formal university- or college-based coursework and even thesis work. Such opportunities are typically highly structured, coherent, multifaceted programs that are essentially achievement oriented. That is, the finishing point is contingent on successful completion of assignments, tasks, and challenges and is normally accompanied by a degree or a certificate. Other formal training opportunities may also be accompanied by a certificate of completion but might best be thought of as participation oriented. That is to say, the finishing point is contingent on successful participation in the program and associated activities without undertaking assignments that, ultimately, would be graded. Finally, training in evaluation happens in many cases informally through incidental learning or learning-by-doing. Evaluators enter the field through a wide range of career paths, many with no formal training. Learning-by-doing may arise through collaborative work on teams, mentoring arrangements, or perhaps in some instances through self-study and trial-and-error.

As shown in Figure 1.1, sources of K/S/A work to enhance the capacity to do evaluation. This would happen first, at the individual, and then at the organizational level, as the transfer of learning takes place. We would argue that for the most part sources of K/S/A would be heavily focused on evaluation methods and practice, although university-based programs might also include curriculum associated with evaluation theory, especially with regard to uses and influences. Sources of K/S/A we see as overlapping with organizational support structures, a second antecedent construct to which we now direct our attention.

Organizational support structures is an antecedent construct in our framework, originally developed by Goh and associates (Goh, 2000; Goh, Quan, & Cousins, 2007; Goh & Richards, 1997) in their work on organizational learning. Organizational structures and supports include low job formalization and the acquisition of relevant and appropriate organizational knowledge and skills by organization members. They are also represented by reward systems, in the form of formal and informal incentive mechanisms, and various communication structures within the organization, which serve to foster the horizontal and vertical flow of knowledge and information. Professional development activities, whether formal or informal, represent yet another organizational support structure. Such activities might be linked in direct ways to evaluation training, hence our representation of overlap with sources of K/S/A.

Organizational support structures are part of a conceptual framework of organizational learning capacity (Goh, 2000), a potential outcome of the capacity to do and use evaluation within the organization. We now turn to an explication of this and other constructs associated with our evaluation capacity framework.

Organizational Capacity to Do and Use Evaluation. Represented within the upper right-hand side of Figure 1.1 are elements associated with the nature of organizational evaluation capacity and associated dimensions. Consequences of such capacity are represented in the lower part of the figure and are described below.

Capacity to do evaluation, as mentioned, arises predominantly from formal and informal training or learning opportunities. Such capacity would reflect the transfer of knowledge and skill from training to workplace applications. Application might take the form of planning and framing evaluation (including evaluation objective setting and framework development); instrument development and validation; ethical considerations; data collection; data processing, analysis, and interpretation; reporting and follow-up; and the like. The capacity to do evaluation would be represented not only by technical procedural knowledge but also by "soft skills," such as conflict resolution, interpersonal dynamics appropriate to cooperative teamwork, facilitation skills, and the like. The development of soft skills is more likely to come from practical experience in doing evaluation—learning-by-doing—as opposed to formal classroom instruction, for example. No doubt such thinking underlies the conscious choice of some university-based programs to include field experience and/or practicum components as part of their curriculum.

Evaluative inquiry is taken to imply the nature of and extent to which evaluation is actually occurring within the organization. Evaluative inquiry might take the form of internally mandated and conducted evaluation projects or those implemented by external evaluators under the oversight of suitably trained organizational personnel. They may include the development of an evaluation framework as a preliminary step, or may rely on planning and framing as part of the evaluation exercise. Depending on organizational information needs, they may be formative or summative in nature; use quantitative, qualitative, or mixed methods; be completely implemented by trained evaluators; or, alternatively, be highly collaborative, even participatory. Evaluations may be comprehensive in their coverage of a program or may roll out over time in a sequenced set of projects. The number of programs evaluated per year, who is involved and in what capacity, would be good indicators of the extent to which evaluative inquiry is happening.

Evaluative inquiry may have direct and/or indirect uses and influences as represented in the framework, but such paths of influence are likely to be mediated by a host of contextual variables and conditions.

Mediating conditions will serve to temper or shape the impact of evaluation within the organization. Such conditions in our framework generally have been identified from research on evaluation use (e.g., Cousins, 2003; Shulha & Cousins, 1997) but more specifically from our own empirical research on evaluation in government (Cousins et al., 2008). Factors and conditions supporting or intruding on organizational uses of evaluation include at least the following: timeliness, constructive nature of feedback, information needs of primary users, credibility of findings, accessibility to primary users, communicability, involvement of nonevaluator stakeholders, and relevance to decision priorities.

Capacity to use evaluation is a construct that reflects the nature of and extent to which evaluation use and influence occurs within the organization (e.g., Cousins et al., 2004; Mark & Henry, 2004; Shulha & Cousins, 1997). To what extent are key program and organizational decision makers savvy with evaluation processes and findings? Planned conscious uses of evaluation findings would include instrumental uses as decision support, whether at the level of program disposition (e.g., termination, continuance, and expansion) or program revision for improvement; conceptual or educational uses reflected by learning and discovery associated with the program itself or the effects (intended, unintended) that it is having; and symbolic or persuasive uses, such as reaffirmation of program worth, compliance with organizational or program sponsor mandates, and the like. The use of findings may be planned and/or conscious, or impact may take the form of serendipitous influence on organizational and program thinking and decision making.

Influence, and indeed use, may also arise from evaluation processes, quite apart from the nature of the findings or content messages coming from the evaluation data. Process use and influence occur through participation or involvement in evaluation, proximity to it or through relationship building between trained evaluators and nonevaluator stakeholders (Cousins, 2007; Forss, Rebien, & Carlsson, 2002; Patton, 1997, 2008). Examples would be the development of knowledge and skill in evaluation logic or the development of an inquiry-minded approach to routine organizational business and processes. Process use may be consciously planned or may arise incidentally through evaluative inquiry or exposure to it.

The capacity to use evaluation, as we suggest in Figure 1.1, will naturally have effects in and of itself within the organization. We now turn to a description of the consequences of evaluation capacity.

Consequences of Organizational Evaluation Capacity. With a focus on integrating evaluation into the organizational culture and evaluation as an organizational learning system, organizational capacity for evaluation naturally relates to organizational learning capacity. We now turn to our description of this construct and where it, in turn, may lead in terms of organizational consequences.

Organizational learning capacity (OLC) is a multifaceted construct composed of key strategic building blocks found in learning organizations. This conception was based on a synthesis and integration of the management literature (Goh, 2000). The strategic building blocks are as follows:

- *Mission and vision.* Clarity and employee support of the mission, strategy, and espoused values of the organization.
- *Leadership.* Leadership that is perceived as empowering employees, encouraging an experimenting culture, and showing strong commitment to the organization.
- *Experimentation.* A strong culture of experimentation that is rewarded and supported at all levels in the organization.
- *Transfer of knowledge.* The ability of an organization to transfer knowledge within and from outside the organization and to learn from failures.
- *Teamwork and cooperation.* An emphasis on teamwork and group problem solving as the mode of operation and for developing innovative ideas.

These building blocks are believed to be mutually supportive and interrelated factors in a learning organization although are displayed as individual dimensions. And, as we have implied, they are understood to rely on organizational structures and supports such as job formalization and the attainment of appropriate information and skills by organization members (Goh & Richards, 1997).

It would not be difficult to imagine that highly developed learning organizations would have, and may have, benefited from a well-developed capacity to use evaluation. The aforementioned building blocks of the learning organization—mission and vision, experimentation, transfer of knowledge, leadership, collaboration, and team work—depend on organizational support structures but are likely to be enhanced through systematic inquiry. Related would be the development of an inquiry habit of mind (Sutherland, 2004). That is, the more an organization experiences successful use of evaluation, the more inclined it would be to engage in such practice. This is consonant with our hypothesis that data use leads to data valuing (Cousins et al., 2005).

Naturally if we think about the learning capacity of an organization, we need to consider potential consequences for the organization. To the extent to which organizations have developed their OLC, differential consequences will be the result.

Organizational consequences of OLC would include, for example, shared mental representations or understandings of the organization and how it operates. Most theorists agree that organizational learning cannot happen in the absence of individual learning by organization members. This multidimensional construct ranges from low-level, first-order, or single-loop learning, where change is incremental, to high-level, second-order, or double-loop learning where fundamental assumptions about the organization and its operation are surfaced, questioned, and ultimately altered (Fiol & Lyles, 1985; Huber, 1991; Lant & Mezias, 1992; Lundberg, 1989).

Having described the conceptual framework to do and use evaluation, we now turn to some thoughts about its potential uses and applications.

Implications for Research and Practice

Our primary interest in developing the framework is to inform research on evaluation as suggested above. In its current form it represents a collection of constructs and tentative relationships among them that might serve to guide instrument development, data collection, data analysis, and interpretation. In essence it will serve to bound research on evaluation capacity within organizations. This is an important contribution because to date much of the conceptual work on evaluation capacity and ECB is based on thin, anecdotal evidence. Nielsen et al. (2011) suggest that much of this evidence is qualitative and does not permit generalizability. In their words: "most contributions are grounded and informed by a qualitative research design driven by case studies, only analytical generalization is possible" (p. 325). We would argue that the evidence base for ECB in general and evaluation capacity in particular is largely based on reflective case narratives, such as individual accounts of ECB efforts (such as Volkov, 2008), or the collection of "case studies" compiled by Compton et al. (2002). Such studies are unquestionably valuable and insightful but they are limited since in the absence of specification of methods, their veracity cannot be evaluated. Yet we have seen recent research on ECB that transcends the limitations of reflective case narratives. Consider, for example, the collection of empirical studies on ECB published in a special issue of the *Canadian Journal of Program Evaluation* (Cousins, 2008). The collection included a mix of quantitative and qualitative studies, virtually all specifying the methods used for systematic inquiry. While we appreciate the argument put forward by Nielsen et al. (2011) for quantitative research, our view is that there is much to be gained from rigorous, defensible qualitative inquiry, particularly given that our conceptual understanding of organizational evaluation capacity is not very well developed.

In our current research program we have simultaneous streams of inquiry. On the one hand, we conducted a pan-Canadian survey of internal evaluators (Cousins et al., 2008) using a hybrid questionnaire that was developed on the basis of Figure 1.1. Data of this sort permit some direct tests of the validity of the framework. Specific relationships can be explored among constructs and paths of influence can be examined. The results of this exploratory analysis showed a pattern of moderately high ratings on organizational learning and support functions, the extent to which evaluation is being conducted and used, and stakeholder involvement in evaluation. Some differences across respondent roles, organization type, and evaluation knowledge were also observed in this study. Further research along these lines is currently underway.

In a related stream, the focus for the current volume, we conducted a multiple case study of eight organizations using Figure 1.1 as an overarching framework for conceptualizing the research. In this qualitative study, we are looking deeply within case organizations in government, the voluntary sector, and educational institutions to understand the forces at play in terms of capacity to do and use evaluation. Our case organizations not only span different sectors but they also include organizations at different stages of development in terms of the capacity to do and especially to use evaluation. The results of the cross-case analyses appearing in Chapter 3 of this volume provide some keen insights into the nature, causes, and consequences of organizational evaluation capacity and will move us further toward understanding how to bring that about.

Other projects that are underway include research intended to understand in deeper ways the nature of process use, factors and conditions that foster it, and the effects that it has (Amo & Cousins, 2012). Another study is directed at the development and validation of a profile framework of organizational capacity to do and use evaluation. Bourgeois and Cousins (2008, 2013) embraced directly the notion that the capacity to use evaluation is an essential element in a broader evaluation capacity framework. They developed and validated a profile-based conceptual framework or multidimensional matrix that framed dimensions of organizational evaluation capacity in terms of levels of capacity development. The dimensions aligned with considerations of the capacity to do evaluation (human resources, organizational resources, evaluation planning, and activities) as well as the capacity to use evaluation (evaluation literacy, organizational decision making, and learning benefits). A tool that organizations can use to plot their evaluation capacity profile is the current focus for this research program (Bourgeois, Toews, Whynot, & Lamarche, 2013).

At present the framework offers only tentative advice for evaluation practice but we would expect that such considerations will be augmented through the development of research-based knowledge. Research in this vein will help us to ground ECB in organizational change theory. Potentially we will be able to offer insights as to not only what high evaluation capacity organizations look like but also how they got that way. Such understanding will move us closer to developing a theory of integration of evaluation into the organizational culture.

Of course, methodologically, many other choices and options remain, with regard to research on ECB. For example, research grounded in narrative inquiry might draw on the framework as basis for analysis and understanding organizational experiences and processes. Or, as an alternative suggestion, network analysis might be employed in a within organization investigation of flows of evaluative knowledge and processes. We are hopeful that this way of conceiving the capacity to do and use evaluation will stimulate others to take up research on evaluation or to provide a basis for interpretation and reflection. We now turn in the next chapter to an explicit application of the framework, our multiple case study of eight organizations.

Note

1. Managed by Unit Nations Children's Fund (UNICEF) and the International Organization for Cooperation in Evaluation (IOCE). Available at http://www.mymande.org/

References

Amo, C., & Cousins, J. B. (2012). *Investigating the relationship between process use and use of evaluation findings in a government context (Working Paper)*. Ottawa, Canada: University of Ottawa.

Baizerman, M., Compton, D., & Stockdill, S. H. (2002). Editors' notes. In D. W. Compton, M. Baizerman, & S. H. Stockdill (Eds.), *New Directions for Evaluation: No. 93. The art, craft and science of evaluation capacity building* (pp. 1–6). San Francisco, CA: Jossey Bass.

Bourgeois, I., & Cousins, J. B. (2008). Informing evaluation capacity building through profiling organizational capacity for evaluation: An empirical examination of four Canadian Federal Government organizations. *Canadian Journal of Program Evaluation, 23*(3), 127–146.

Bourgeois, I., & Cousins, J. B. (2013). Understanding dimensions of organizational evaluation capacity. *American Journal of Evaluation, 34*(3), 299–319.

Bourgeois, I., Toews, E., Whynot, J., & Lamarche, M. K. (2013). Measuring organizational evaluation capacity in the Canadian Federal Government. *Canadian Journal of Program Evaluation, 28*(2), 1–19.

Carman, J. G., & Fredericks, K. A. (2010). Evaluation capacity and non-profit organizations: Is the glass half-empty or half-full? *American Journal of Evaluation, 31*(1), 81–104.

Compton, D., Baizerman, M., & Stockdill, S. H. (Eds.). (2002). *New Directions for Evaluation: No. 93. The art, craft and science of evaluation capacity building*. San Francisco, CA: Jossey-Bass.

Cousins, J. B. (2003). Utilization effects of participatory evaluation. In T. Kellaghan, D. L. Stufflebeam & L. A. Wingate (Eds.), *International handbook of educational evaluation* (pp. 245–265). Boston, MA: Kluwer.

Cousins, J. B. (2007). *New Directions for Evaluation: No. 116. Process use in theory, research and practice*. San Francisco, CA: Jossey-Bass.

Cousins, J. B. (Ed.). (2008). Understanding organizational capacity for evaluation [Special Issue]. *Canadian Journal of Program Evaluation, 23*(3).

Cousins, J. B., & Aubry, T. (2006). *Roles for government in evaluation quality assurance: Discussion paper*. Ottawa, Canada: Treasury Board Secretariat of Canada and University of Ottawa.

Cousins, J. B., & Chouinard, J. (2012). *Participatory evaluation up close: A review and integration of research-based knowledge*. Charlotte, NC: Information Age Press.

Cousins, J. B., & Earl, L. (1995). *Participatory evaluation in education: Studies in evaluation use and organizational learning*. London: Falmer.

Cousins, J. B., Elliott, C., Amo, C., Bourgeois, I., Chouinard, J. A., Goh, S. C., & Lahey, R. (2008). Organizational capacity to do and use evaluation: Results of a pan-Canadian survey of evaluators. *Canadian Journal of Program Evaluation, 23*(3), 1–35.

Cousins, J. B., Goh, S., & Clark, S. (2005). Data use leads to data valuing: Evaluative inquiry for school decision making. *Leadership and Policy in Schools, 4*, 155–176.

Cousins, J. B., Goh, S., Clark, S., & Lee, L. (2004). Integrating evaluative inquiry into the organizational culture: A review and synthesis of the knowledge base. *Canadian Journal of Program Evaluation, 19*(2), 99–141.

Engle, M., & Altschuld, J. W. (2003). An update on university-based evaluation training. *Evaluation Exchange, 9*(4), 13.

Engle, M., Altschuld, J. W., & Kim, Y. C. (2006). 2002 survey of evaluation preparation programs in universities: An update of the 1992 American evaluation association-sponsored study. *American Journal of Evaluation, 27*(3), 353–359.

Fiol, C. M., & Lyles, M. A. (1985). Organizational learning. *Academy of Management Review, 10,* 803–813.

Fleischer, D. N., Christie, C. A., & LaVelle, K. B. (2008). Perceptions of evaluation capacity building in the United States: A descriptive study of American Evaluation Association members. *Canadian Journal of Program Evaluation, 23*(3), 37–60.

Forss, K., Kruse, S.-E., Taut, S., & Tenden, E. (2006). Chasing a ghost? An essay on participatory evaluation and capacity development. *Evaluation, 12*(10), 128–144.

Forss, K., Rebien, C. C., & Carlsson, J. (2002). Process use of evaluation: Types of use that precede lessons learned and feedback. *Evaluation, 8*(1), 29–45.

Garcia-Iriarte, E., Suarez-Balcazar, Y., Taylor-Ritzler, T., & Luna, M. (2011). A catalyst-for-change approach to evaluation capacity building. *American Journal of Evaluation, 32*(2), 168–182.

Goh, S. C. (2000). Towards a learning organization. The strategic building blocks. *SAM Advanced Management Journal, 63*(2), 15–22.

Goh, S. C., Quan, T. K., & Cousins, J. B. (2007). The organizational learning survey: A re-evaluation of unidimensionality. *Psychological Reports, 101,* 707–721.

Goh, S. C., & Richards, G. (1997). Benchmarking the learning capacity of organizations. *European Management Journal, 15*(5), 575–583.

Henry, G. T., & Mark, M. M. (2003). Beyond use: Understanding evaluation's influence on attitudes and actions. *American Journal of Evaluation, 24,* 293–314.

Huber, G. P. (1991). Organizational learning: The contribution processes and the literature. *Organization Science, 2,* 88–115.

King, J. A., Stevahn, L., Ghere, G., & Minnema, J. (2001). Toward a taxonomy of essential evaluation competencies. *American Journal of Evaluation, 22,* 229–247.

Kirkhart, K. (2000). Reconceptualizing evaluation use: An integrated theory of influence. In V. Carcelli & H. Preskill (Eds.), *New Directions for Evaluation: No. 88. The expanding scope of evaluation use* (pp. 5–23). San Francisco, CA: Jossey-Bass.

Labin, S., Duffy, J. L., Meyers, D. C., Wandersman, A., & Lesesne, C. A. (2012). A research synthesis of the evaluation capacity building literature. *American Journal of Evaluation, 33,* 307–338.

Lant, T. K., & Mezias, S. J. (1992). An organizational learning model of convergence and reorientation. *Organization Science, 3,* 47–71.

Lawrenz, F., Thomas, K., Huffman, D., & Covington Clarkson, L. (2008). Evaluation capacity building in the schools: Administrator-led and teacher-led perspectives. *Canadian Journal of Program Evaluation, 23*(3), 61–82.

Lundberg, C. C. (1989). On organizational learning: Implications and opportunities for exapnding organizational development. *Research in Organizational Change and Development, 3,* 61–82.

Mark, M. M., & Henry, G. T. (2004). The mechanisms and outcomes of evaluation influence. *Evaluation, 10,* 35–57.

Milstein, B., & Cotton, D. (2000, October). *Defining concepts for the presidential strand on building evaluation capacity.* Paper presented at the 2000 meeting of the American Evaluation Association, Honolulu, Hawaii.

Nacarrella, L., Pirkis, J., Kohn, F., Morley, B., Burgess, P., & Blashki, G. (2007). Building evaluation capacity: Definitional and practical implications from an Australian case study. *Evaluation and Program Planning, 30*(3), 231–236.

Nielsen, S. B., Lemire, S., & Skov, M. (2011). Measuring evaluation capacity—Results and implications of a Danish study. *American Journal of Evaluation, 32*(3), 324–344.

Owen, J., & Lambert, K. (1995). Roles for evaluators in learning organizations. *Evaluation, 1,* 237–250.

Patton, M. Q. (1997). *Utilization-focused evaluation: A new century text* (3rd ed.). Thousand Oaks, CA: Sage.

Patton, M. Q. (2008). *Utilization-focused evaluation* (4th ed.). Thousand Oaks, CA: Sage.

Patton, M. Q. (2011). *Developmental evaluation: Applying complexity concepts to enhance innovation and use.* New York, NY: Guilford.

Preskill, H., & Boyle, S. (2008). A multidisciplinary model of evaluation capacity building. *American Journal of Evaluation, 29*(4), 443–459.

Preskill, H., & Russ-Eft, D. (2005). *Building evaluation capacity: 72 activities for teaching and training.* Thousand Oaks, CA: Sage.

Preskill, H., & Torres, R. T. (1999). *Evaluative inquiry for learning in organizations.* Thousand Oaks. CA: Sage.

Sanders, J. R. (2003). Mainstreaming evaluation. In J. J. Barnette & J. R. Sanders (Eds.), *New Directions for Evaluation: No. 99. The mainstreaming of evaluation* (pp. 3–6). San Francisco, CA: Jossey-Bass.

Shulha, L. M., & Cousins, J. B. (1997). Evaluation use: Theory, research and practice since 1986. *Evaluation Practice, 18*, 195–208.

Stevahn, L., King, J. A., Ghere, G., & Minnema, J. (2005a). Establishing essential competencies for program evaluators. *American Journal of Evaluation, 26*, 43–59.

Stevahn, L., King, J. A., Ghere, G., & Minnema, J. (2005b). Evaluator competencies in university-based training programs. *Canadian Journal of Program Evaluation, 20*(2), 101–123.

Stockdill, S. H., Baizerman, M., & Compton, D. (2002). Toward a definition of the ECB process: A conversation with the ECB literature. In D. Compton, M. Baizerman, & S. H. Stockdill (Eds.), *New Directions in Evaluation: No. 93. The art, craft and science of evaluation capacity building* (pp. 7–25). San Francisco, CA: Jossey-Bass.

Sutherland, S. (2004). Creating a culture of data use for continuous improvement: A case study of an Edison Project School. *American Journal of Evaluation, 25*, 277–293.

Volkov, B. (2008). A bumpy journey to evaluation capacity: A case study of evaluation capacity building in a private foundation. *Canadian Journal of Program Evaluation, 23*(3), 175–197.

Zorzi, R., Perrin, B., McGuire, M., Long, B., & Lee, L. (2002). Defining the benefits, outputs, and knowledge elements of program evaluation. *Canadian Journal of Program Evaluation, 17*(3), 143–150.

J. BRADLEY COUSINS *is a professor of educational evaluation at the Faculty of Education and Director of the Centre for Research on Educational and Community Services (CRECS), University of Ottawa.*

SWEE C. GOH *is Professor Emeritus in organizational behavior at the Telfer School of Management, University of Ottawa, Canada.*

CATHERINE J. ELLIOTT *is an assistant professor in the Telfer School of Management at the University of Ottawa.*

ISABELLE BOURGEOIS *is a professor of program evaluation at l'École nationale d'administration publique (National School of Public Administration), University of Québec, Gatineau, Québec.*

Cousins, J. B., Bourgeois, I., & Associates. (2014). Multiple case study methods and findings. In J. B. Cousins & I. Bourgeois (Eds.), *Organizational capacity to do and use evaluation. New Directions for Evaluation, 141*, 25–99.

2

Multiple Case Study Methods and Findings

J. Bradley Cousins, Isabelle Bourgeois, and Associates

Abstract

Research on organizational evaluation capacity building (ECB) has focused very much on the capacity to do evaluation, neglecting organizational demand for evaluation and the capacity to use it. This qualitative multiple case study comprises a systematic examination of organizational capacity within eight distinct organizations guided by a common conceptual framework. Described in this chapter are the rationale and methods for the study and then the sequential presentation of findings for each of the eight case organizations. Data collection and analyses for these studies occurred six years ago; findings are cross-sectional and do not reflect changes in organizations or their capacity for evaluation since that time. The format for presenting the findings was standardized so as to foster cross-case analyses, the focus for the next and final chapter of this volume. © Wiley Periodicals, Inc., and the American Evaluation Association.

Purpose and Rationale

In Chapter 1, we introduced a conceptual framework that can help guide research on organizational evaluation capacity. That framework includes as an integral element the capacity to use evaluation as well as the capacity to do it. As Nielsen, Lemire, and Skov (2011) have noted, many studies of ECB are focused on the practice of capacity building while few have focused more directly on organizational capacity itself. It is imperative to learn more about what that capacity looks like in order to better inform strategies, practices, processes, and the like, designed to improve it.

The excellent review and integration of cases of ECB by Labin, Duffy, Meyers, Wandersman, and Lesesne (2012) is perhaps the most systematic review of empirical work in the area published to date. The "integrative framework" used to organize the review is relatively comprehensive and includes elements that touch on antecedent conditions and influences, the nature of ECB practice and consequences or outcomes arising from ECB initiatives. Such consequences are of central interest in the present study because they touch on organizational capacity for evaluation. Labin et al. (2012) break this category into different units of analysis and aspects: changes at the individual, organizational, and program level; negative outcomes; and lessons learned. The category overlaps with our interest in organizational capacity for evaluation but much more along the lines of the capacity to do evaluation, as opposed to the organizational capacity to use evaluation. Our sense is that their interest in the organization's use of evaluation has more to do with use of evaluation methods and practices per se than it does with organizational capacity to use evaluation findings, and process use, whether defined at the individual, group, or organizational level.

The present multiple case study aims to deepen our understanding about the integration of evaluation into organizational culture through the presentation of a coherent collection of organizational case studies on evaluation capacity. The studies were guided by the conceptual framework delineated in Chapter 1, which was codeveloped by members of the research team who participated in the multiple case study and other aspects of our research program (e.g., concept mapping study, quantitative survey of internal evaluators; see Cousins et al., 2008). The study adds to our knowledge about organizational capacity to do and use evaluation quite apart from ECB processes, practices, and strategies. Clearly, the organizations that we included were all engaged in ECB practices at some level, and we noted some diversity in approaches. But our central focus was on the construct of evaluation capacity itself. The study was designed to explore what such capacity looks like in practice and the forces and factors at play in shaping such capacity. Our specific research questions were the following:

1. What is the nature of organizational capacity to *do* and *use* evaluation?
2. What are the factors and conditions that influence the integration of evaluation into the organizational culture?

Secondarily we also had an interest in ECB within these organizations. We wanted to know about strategies they used to develop their capacity to do and use evaluation. We now turn to a description of the methods employed in the research including criteria for sample selection.

Study Methods

First we describe our general methodological approach to the research and then provide details about our sampling strategy and the organizations that we included in the study.

Methodological Approach

The study is qualitative but guided very directly by the conceptual framework depicted in Chapter 1 of this volume (see Figure 1.1). In this respect, we subscribe to the general orientation to research put forward by Miles and Huberman (1994). The study is not designed to validate the conceptual framework we developed. Rather, it is intended to profit from that framework in terms of the identification and explication of boundaries for the inquiry. The framework is intended as a collection of variables or constructs and suggested relations among them. We used it to inform the development of interview protocols and to guide analysis and interpretation. While used as a guide to inquiry, the framework does not preclude the inclusion of emergent variables and relationships.

The study is a multiple case study meaning that it is a collection of investigations into selected case organizations. The study design is cross-sectional and data were collected in 2007. Our purpose is to describe and explore the phenomenon of organizational capacity to do and use evaluation by investigating it within its real-life context. But the study is also explanatory in that we look for causal relationships among variables of interest. Descriptive, exploratory, and explanatory analyses are part and parcel of the case organization reports appearing in this section. In the next section, we look across cases for common patterns as well as points of divergence. At some level, cross-case analyses contribute to our understanding about the extent to which study findings are generalizable, yet this is not the purpose of the inquiry. Our central interest remains developing a deeper understanding of the complexities of organizational evaluation capacity than is currently the case. We leave to the reader the question of how well the findings travel to other organizations. Further, despite data collection some years ago, we did not examine patterns of change in organizational evaluation capacity over time. Our findings must be understood to be cross-sectional at a particular window in time.

Sample—Case Organizations

Case organizations for the research were nominated by members of our research team on the basis of two central criteria. First, the organization had to be in the public sector (including voluntary organizations) and second and most important, the organization had to have a significant interest in the implementation and use of evaluation. Secondarily, for logistical reasons, the organization had to be located within the Ottawa region or a reasonable distance from it. We did not require that organizations had developed to a particular level of maturity with respect to their engagement with evaluation.

A range of organizations were considered on the basis of personal contact and experience with them by members of the research team. Ultimately, decisions as to which organizations to invite were made collectively by the research group. Informal contact with known organizational contact persons was made by respective research team members and a formal letter of invitation (detailing purposes, expectations, timing, etc.) was shared. Contact persons then formally agreed and notified the research team. In the end, we invited eight organizations and all agreed to participate. Table 2.1 provides a brief overview of the selected organizations.

As can be seen in Table 2.1, the organizations cover a broad range of professional practice including an education institution, community mental health and health nongovernmental organizations (NGOs), donor agencies in international development and social/community improvement, and federal government (human resources, and revenue and taxation). The breadth of the sample reflects evaluation's interdisciplinary character. The organizations were mostly located in Ottawa with one in Montreal and two in Toronto. They vary quite enormously in terms of size and annual budget with scope ranging from international to national, provincial, and regional.

As mentioned, organizations were selected mostly because of their interest in evaluation as an organizational strategy. Most had formal evaluation departments or units, while other, particularly smaller organizations, relied on organization members with evaluation responsibility or to some extent on external partnerships with the university sector. The cases are described in more detail below as a preamble to the presentation of findings.

Data Collection

Teams of varying configurations accepted responsibility for all aspects of data collection, analysis, and reporting for specific cases (see author lists associated with respective cases below). The within-organization research design comprised the two phases described below. Phase 1 involved the development of understanding about the organizations' capacity for evaluation and Phase 2 was a follow-up validation process. We used this qualitative design with some success in prior research on evaluation capacity in schools (Cousins, Goh, & Clark, 2005). In virtually all cases researchers followed the research protocol; minor exceptions are noted below within the respective presentations of findings.

Phase 1: Development. *Review of documentation.* First, members of the research team familiarized themselves with the case organization by reviewing relevant public domain documentation available on websites. This included organizational structure, mission, history, and reports such as strategic plans, sample evaluations, and research studies. The research

Table 2.1. Descriptive Characteristics of Case Organizations

Organization	Sector	Objectives and Activities	Number of Full-Time Equivalent Employees	Annual Budget[a]	Scope of Activities	Responsibility for Evaluation	Formal (External) Evaluation Requirements
1. Dawson College (Montreal)	Education, postsecondary	English-language College under CEGEP[b] system in Quebec; offers technical, employment-oriented programs, as well as preuniversity preparation	600 employees (faculty and staff)	$63 million	Provincial	Evaluation Manager position supported internal evaluation efforts	Evaluation requirements from the Quebec provincial government
2. Canadian Mental Health Association, Ottawa Branch (Ottawa)	Not-for-profit, community mental health	Social action, education, community service, and research on mental health issues	100 case workers	$15 million	Regional; serves Ottawa area clients and organizations	In-house evaluations as well as university-led evaluation activities	Accountable to CMHA Ontario, partner agency in the CMHA national network.
3. International Development Research Centre (Ottawa)	Federal government, international development (Crown Corporation)	Supporting applied research of direct benefit to developing countries and their citizen	450 employees located in Ottawa and in six regional offices around the world	$170 million	International: developing nations	Evaluation unit headed by a director employed approximately six full-time employees; support provided by the private sector	Not subject to the TBS[c] policy on evaluation but has instituted its own formal evaluation structure and requirements

Continued

Table 2.1. Continued

Organization	Sector	Objectives and Activities	Number of Full-Time Equivalent Employees	Annual Budget[a]	Scope of Activities	Responsibility for Evaluation	Formal (External) Evaluation Requirements
4. Canadian Cancer Society (Ottawa)	Not-for-profit, health (charitable organization)	Research, information, prevention, advocacy, and support services targeted for those affected by cancer	1,200 employees	$180 million	National	External evaluation conducted by the Propel Centre for Population Health Impact (University of Waterloo)	Not applicable, accountable to donors
5. Canada Revenue Agency (Ottawa)	Federal government, revenue and taxation	Administration of tax laws for most provinces and territories as well as benefits and incentive programs delivered through the tax system	40,000 employees located in Ottawa as well as in regional offices across the country	$3 billion	National	Program evaluation division (within the Audit and Evaluation Directorate) with approximately 15 employees; most evaluation work conducted in-house	2009 TBS policy on evaluation requires the evaluation of 100% of direct program spending within a five-year cycle
6. Human Resources & Skills Development Canada (Ottawa)	Federal government, Human resource development	Responsible for labor market and income support programming, including employment insurance and postsecondary skill development[d]	24,000 employees located in Ottawa as well as in regional offices across the country	$100 billion	National	Program evaluation division within the Audit and Evaluation Directorate); approximately 55 employees with planning and oversight responsibility	2009 TBS policy on evaluation requires the evaluation of 100% of direct program spending within a five-year cycle

Continued

Table 2.1. Continued

Organization	Sector	Objectives and Activities	Number of Full-Time Equivalent Employees	Annual Budget[a]	Scope of Activities	Responsibility for Evaluation	Formal (External) Evaluation Requirements
7. United Way of Greater Toronto (Toronto)	Not-for-profit, community development (charitable organization)	Neighborhood and community development; social research, public policy, capacity building, strategic initiatives	170 employees, 150 member agencies, 50 plus grant recipient agencies	$120 million	Regional: Greater Toronto Area	Office of organizational capacity building, sector specific evaluation personnel	Not applicable, accountable to donors
8. Trillium Foundation of Ontario (Toronto)	Para-governmental	Grantmaking foundation responsible for investments into community-building initiatives	Approximately 100 employees (two thirds are located in Toronto, the remainder in regional offices across Ontario)	$100 million	Provincial	Policy, Research, and Evaluation Unit (six employees in total) responsible for externally contracted studies; evaluation comprised approximately 20% of group's total activities	Ontario Provincial Government

[a]Wherever possible, the annual budget presented in the table is for FY 2006–2007 or 2007–2008, in order to better contextualize the findings included in each of the cases. However, data were not available for all organizations for those FYs; in such cases, the annual budget for the closest FY was included in the table.

[b]CEGEP is Collège d'enseignement général et professionnel, known officially in English as a "General and Vocational College."

[c]TBS is Treasury Board Secretariat of Canada.

[d]Note that in Canada education is a provincial matter partially funded through federal transfer payments. HRSDC engages in postsecondary skill development outside of the institutional postsecondary system.

team leader negotiated with the organizational contact person to identify organization members to interview and mutually convenient times for individual interviews. Identified organization members included senior organization decision makers, other decision makers, and those responsible for the evaluation function within the organization. Table 2.2 provides a summary of who was interviewed at each organization.

Individual interviews. Members of the research team identified a sample of individuals with some knowledge of the organizational evaluation function over the last few years—either as producers and/or users of evaluation. These individuals were invited to participate in an individual interview with a member(s) of the research team. They were furnished in advance with a letter of informed consent detailing the purpose and expectations for participation in the study. Interviews were conducted on-site and were audiotaped, with the participant's permission. The interviews were semistructured and guided by a common interview schedule.[1] During the interview period, additional documents were collected if they were deemed relevant. However, the primary focus for data collection in this phase was the individual interview. In some cases, more than one person was interviewed simultaneously. The researchers tried to discourage this but sometimes this was necessary due to logistics.

Draft Case Profile Report. In most cases, individual interviews were summarized afterward by the researcher who had done the interview. The summaries were constructed while listening to the audio recordings and included a healthy sampling of verbatim quotations. Interview and document data were then analyzed by the research team according to the main themes of data collection. Again, this step of the process was informed by the conceptual framework (Figure 1.1, Chapter 1). A *Case Profile Report* was then drafted typically by the lead researcher for each team. The reports were approximately 10 pages in length, single spaced. Across cases a common report structure was used to foster comparability. The report was revised on the basis of review and feedback of other team members who had been involved in the data collection for the respective case. The draft was also shared with members of the wider research team for comment. A final version of the draft Phase 1 Case Profile Report was then prepared for sharing with members of the organization through the contact person.

Report distribution. The report was then shared as a draft and on a confidential basis with the respective organization's contact person. A few copies were sent in hardcopy format but the contact person was also sent an electronic version. Contact persons were asked to share the report with interested organization members in preparation for Phase 2.

Phase 2: Validation. *Focus group.* After having had an opportunity to review the draft report, individuals were invited, through the contact person, to participate in a focus group. The purpose of the focus group was to discuss the report, validate it, and/or otherwise add value and understanding. We developed a brief protocol for the focus group meeting,[2] which was

Table 2.2. Participants Interviewed in Phase 1 by Case Organization

Case Organization	N	Roles
1. Dawson College	12	Director General, the Dean of Program Services & International Development, the Evaluation Manager, six administrators and three teachers.
2. Canadian Mental Health Association	7	Agency director, program directors with evaluation responsibility, agency middle managers and other personnel.
3. International Development Research Centre	9	CEO and one other senior manager, director, program managers, senior program officer, the evaluation officers. Four persons worked within the evaluation unit.
4. Canadian Cancer Society	9	Chief Executive Officer and the President of the National Board of Directors, members of the Board of Directors (two), divisional executive directors (two), the director of the organization's main external evaluator and program directors/managers (two).
5. Canadian Revenue Agency	12	Director General, Audit and Evaluation; Acting Director, Program Evaluation Division; three program evaluation managers; three program evaluation team leaders; three assistant commissioners; and deputy assistant commissioner.
6. Human Resources and Skills Development Canada	9	Assistant deputy minister level (one), the director general level (two), and the director level (six). Two of the directors interviewed each represented a user group that works with evaluation staff on an ongoing basis.
7. United Way of Greater Toronto	12	Senior managers, manager of organizational capacity building, program directors, program staff, evaluators, member organization representatives.
8. Trillium Foundation	16	CEO, two directors, 11 managers, and two senior staff from across the province.

intended to be relatively unstructured and free-flowing. In Phase 2, we tried to encourage all organization members who had been interviewed to attend but this was usually not possible. We also permitted the inclusion of other interested organization members to attend the meetings. Everyone coming to the meeting was expected to have read over the draft report. It became evident to us that members read over the report with varying levels of intensity but invariably some members of the group had read it closely.

We were not able to arrange Phase 2 focus groups at all participating organizations. In the few cases where focus groups did not occur the research team engaged with the organization contact person for input and comment on the draft case profile. Contact persons were asked to circulate the document to other members, obtain input and feedback, and integrate feedback across organization members for communication with the research team.

Following the focus groups and/or exchanges with contact persons, the Case Profile Report was finalized and we requested acknowledgement from the contact person that it was satisfactory to the organization. The final revised report was then printed and sent to each organization for its own internal uses; an electronic copy was also provided. Organization members understood also that the research team would be using the Case Profile Reports as a basis for conducting cross-case analyses.

We now turn to a presentation of the findings for each organizational case study. The studies are presented in the arbitrary order in which they appear in Tables 2.1 and 2.2. We are indebted to the following research team members for their leadership and intellectual direction on respective studies of case organizations: Courtney Amo, Tim Aubry, Jill A. Chouinard, Catherine Elliott, Anna Engman, Swee C. Goh, Keiko Kuji-Shikatani, Robert Lahey, and Steve Montague. The authors responsible for each case study are identified in the pages that follow.

Case 1: Dawson College

Catherine J. Elliott, J. Bradley Cousins, Swee C. Goh

Introduction and Study Context

Dawson College is the largest English college in the Quebec CEGEP[3] system, with approximately 10,000 students, enrolled in more than 50 fields of study. Offering both technical and preuniversity programs, the College recognizes its dual responsibility to *"prepare students for further academic education and for immediate employment"* and thereby *"contribute to the intellectual, economic and social development of our society"* (excerpt from mission statement). Founded in 1969, the College has expanded from fairly humble beginnings to become a recognized leader in the CEGEP network. This maturity is reflected in its strategic plan in which the College continues to move ahead to tackle new challenges; as noted by one participant, the plan articulates a "clear commitment to dedicate resources to more efficiency, more transparency and to cope with the challenge of accountability."

Faculty and administrators alike express great pride in their organization: "It is a strong community and people are proud to work and study here." There is a clear commitment to student learning which permeates all levels and functions; and a collegial atmosphere in which employees feel that their input is welcome. Yet the decision-making process at Dawson is quite structured and layered and consequently change is not quick. There was some mention that decision making and communication seemed to be becoming less hierarchal and more open than previously was the case. "The new [Director General] and Academic Dean are encouraging much openness in communication."

Dawson has become increasingly proactive with regard to the integration of evaluation processes in recent years. The College integrated evaluation into the operational planning processes and there has been a concerted effort to raise the profile of evaluation in the organization and build capacity to conduct evaluation aided by the hiring of a professional evaluator—the Evaluation Manager—in 2002. Yet program evaluation is still largely seen to be resource-intensive and onerous, an event that analyzes activities that occurred 2–3 years in the past: *"so it is a bit disconnected."* As a result, Dawson launched an *ongoing* process to make evaluation more connected to employees. By engaging organizational members in the process of developing an institutional evaluation policy, the College hopes to make evaluation more timely and relevant, build evaluation capacity, encourage personnel to integrate evaluation into their daily operations, and eventually instill a culture of *ongoing* evaluation. "Ongoing evaluation will make our program evaluations much smoother, much more timely, and with more buy-in...and people won't look at it and think 'this is so much work'."

NEW DIRECTIONS FOR EVALUATION • DOI: 10.1002/ev

Drivers for Evaluation

Several motivators for evaluation were identified by College staff but perhaps most powerful, at least initially, were external pressures and forces. Systematic program evaluation was introduced into the College in 1993, primarily spurred on by the *Commission d'évaluation de l'enseignement collégial du Québec* (CEEC), but also by internal interest in performance evaluation. But at this time there was also a change in Ministry of Education philosophy, which had an enormous impact on the CEGEP system. Whereas before 1993, the faculty operated as "experts" in fairly self-contained departments or disciplines, the emphasis changed to a program approach. This was more holistic and focused more on student outcomes, requiring a significant change in perspective. As a result, the first program evaluation (social sciences) commissioned by the CEEC with this new philosophy proved to be traumatic for the College, a "wake-up call." As one member put it "It was clear out of that evaluation that this wasn't really a program, that it was still a cafeteria approach."

Over the last 10–14 years, the CEEC has introduced reforms to which Dawson must comply and which directly or indirectly involve program evaluation. These include: policy development, program revisions (e.g., competency-based approach), student success plans, strategic plans, and institutional evaluation. However, the majority of respondents were quick to point out the associated benefits of performing these CEEC-mandated evaluations. For example, as one respondent noted, they can stimulate important program revisions: "we saw it as a unique opportunity to make some shifts, some changes in the way we delivered our product." Ongoing internal evaluation activities are guided by Dawson's institutional program evaluation policy (IPEP) that recognizes an ongoing program development cycle. The policy reflects the new Director General's commitment to ongoing evaluation as a basis for decision making. Such activities assist the College in identifying need for program revisions, implementation monitoring, and meeting other information needs: "We now have a policy on program evaluation and we want to make it more efficient"; "ongoing evaluation became something that we wanted to do ..."

Capacity to Do Evaluation

The evaluation unit at Dawson is small but "mighty." In 2002, after a number of years of hiring technical expertise from outside, Dawson made a commitment to establishing a dedicated internal evaluation unit with a full-time professional evaluator. This professional role is multifaceted—to oversee the evaluation process, serve as technical expert, facilitator, coach, and guide—the evaluator "abilitates" others. Depending upon the capabilities of the team, the evaluator also gets intimately involved in the evaluation itself—writing, editing, and analyzing data.

NEW DIRECTIONS FOR EVALUATION • DOI: 10.1002/ev

Often with an internal evaluation model there can be concerns about lack of objectivity and credibility. However, this was not mentioned once by any of the participants. It seems that any such concerns are offset by Dawson's extensive vetting process, by the integrity of the data and evaluation process, the use of multiple sources of evidence, and the seriousness with which the results are treated. As one participant put it:

> There are so many checks and balances. Anyone with self-interest would not be able to get away with it. Evaluations are vetted by the Senate and the Board. They are scrutinized at multiple levels.

For program evaluation, Dawson's process is outlined in the institutional program evaluation policy (IPEP). First, an evaluation committee is struck, with representatives from different constituencies. A smaller group (the writing committee) is then identified and a writer assigned. (The writer is typically a teacher who is allocated release time.) The writing committee does most of the real work associated with the evaluation – design, instrument development, data collection, analysis and report writing. The final report and recommendations are discussed and approved by the evaluation committee and further discussed and approved at multiple levels. An action plan is prepared by the Academic Dean and the Sector Dean is responsible for its implementation. Evaluation at Dawson was highly participative, with 100% of employees involved; there was some variation across different program evaluations in how stakeholders are involved. Students, alumni, and employers are typically sources of data whereas Dawson employees are either directly involved or in roles of advisory/approval.

Despite a general sense of valuing of evaluation, room for growth was a sentiment expressed with regard to resident knowledge and skill about evaluation logic and methods. Overall, interviewees felt that there is a range of skills and knowledge, from "expert" to "none": "There's probably a mixture. There's a small core of quite good people who could do it, but probably a lot of people who wouldn't even know how to approach it." As another interviewee put it:

> In terms of the global population of Dawson, I think that the skill levels are fairly low, but I don't see that as a negative thing. They just need the tools to know how to pull the right information out for evaluation. Right now those tools are very sketchy...

Sources of Evaluation Knowledge

Overwhelmingly, participants emphasized the critical role played by the "expert" evaluation unit, to coach and advise them through the process. The professional evaluator and other evaluation team members are seen to be experienced, professional, and responsive:

... until we had [the Evaluation Manager] and until we had Dawson's (evaluation) department, very, very small. People might be able to do an anecdotal evaluation or even a small questionnaire, but to really tie things together to make it meaningful ... it is difficult.

A second resource person who was consistently cited as vital to the process was the Head of Institutional Research, particularly during the instrument design process.

Consistent with the results above, the principal means by which capacity is built at Dawson is actual involvement in the evaluation process. The participants agreed that there is no replacement for experience. Even teachers, who were familiar with course evaluations and performance appraisal, found the need to differentiate between these types of assessment and program evaluation: "evaluating a course, obviously, assessment. There are certain things that they have in common. But to get into statistics like we did ... we just don't do that with a course."

The ECB model at Dawson College also involves ongoing support. By providing an internal professional evaluation unit—albeit small—those users who get involved in program evaluation can learn in a supportive environment, with expert coaching. In this way, they experience success and the institution expands its overall capacity, while meeting its management objectives and reporting/accountability requirements. The process can also spawn a new (user) champion for evaluation. Recognizing this potential benefit, the Evaluation Manager had recently asked experienced program evaluators–teachers to serve as informal mentors to those who are new to the process. Once again, this can help build capacity.

Other tools and resources that help build capacity (or support its use) include the online systems for data retrieval and guidelines provided by Dawson and the CEEC. In fact, in the early days of evaluation in the CEGEP system, the CEEC focused a great deal of energy on developing resources for Colleges which were in embryonic stages of evaluation. Colleges can now obtain online reports on the standard program indicators—graduation, retention, employment, course success, although user friendliness is somewhat of an issue.

Although this "experiential learning" model of ECB seems to be working well, an ongoing challenge becomes the sustainability of knowledge. Capacity that is built through participation in program evaluation can be lost over time. As suggested by these respondents:

It's a really big learning curve every single time ...

The long term sustainability of evaluation, I'm still not sure of. Evaluation can be done and forgotten in 10 minutes.

It's funny because we have a lot of experience in doing evaluation as an institution, but every time that we start a new program evaluation, we go from scratch.

Ongoing evaluation is largely a response to sustainability concerns. By increasing the degree of employee engagement in the process itself, and by creating a system that can be used on an ongoing basis, there is hope that employees will have ownership over the end result and experience the benefits firsthand, in their own frame of reference and everyday jobs. In short, there is optimism that ongoing evaluation will help build a culture of evaluation at Dawson.

Capacity to Use Evaluation

Dawson College had a relatively long history—over 10 years—of taking program evaluation seriously and acting upon the results. Evaluation findings had been used for decision making—decisions about program development, resource allocation, and program continuation or closure. There is a formal process to follow up in place within the organization: an action plan is prepared by the Academic Dean (in consultation with the Sector Dean and/or Coordinator); and it identifies the specific steps to be taken to address each recommendation in the evaluation report. In addition, the CEEC follows up to ensure action plans are implemented and the Senate pays very close attention to evaluations which are CEEC-mandated and those surrounding which difficult program decisions must be made.

Results are primarily used for program revisions, including significant changes and even program closure as expressed by these staff members:

It isn't a dry exercise with no long term results...there are actual changes that are made as a result of evaluation to various programs.

Evaluation leads to a revision...It either creates minor changes or a complete revision of a program that's been given.

Sometimes the evaluation just formalizes what is already suspected; but in most cases, it also unearths new and interesting findings:

Most of the faculty likely knew already that something needed to change, but they weren't sure what, or how to make it happen.

When we were evaluated in a formal setting, it was a very rigorous process. It helped us look under those "rocks" that we hadn't looked under in a while.

Evaluation findings are generally seen to support change and positive improvement. However, some push back was noted: some staff were concerned that it will "put the death nail in the coffin" of their programs; others fear that they will be scrutinized—"looking with a microscope at what they are doing."

The respondents identified four other consequences that they have observed at Dawson: increased recognition and pride in programs, leverage for additional resources, identification of new issues, and improved accountability and capacity.

Through ongoing evaluation, process use is a naturally occurring phenomenon at Dawson. Learning by doing was a theme echoed by several college staff who had participated in evaluation work:

> Going through it once gives you a better understanding of what you should do the next time and expands your understanding of the process, absolutely.

> Yes, it was positive for me. I met new people in the College and developed an increased respect for people and their different jobs. I personally learned so much more about evaluation.

However, as one individual noted, the breadth of impact was limited to those who were more closely involved in the program evaluation. This observation bodes well for ongoing evaluation, as the process is far more participative than was the prior approach to program evaluation.

Evaluation Enablers and Barriers

We identified four primary enablers of the integration of evaluation into the organizational culture. Firstly, staff described the importance of having demonstrated commitment to evaluation by senior management. Since the beginning, Dawson's senior administration has "valued the act of evaluation and what it could bring to the institution"; they have supported evaluation and dedicated resources to ensuring its success. Most recently, the Director General has championed the ongoing evaluation process and the Academic Dean has restructured operations to bring program evaluation and development closer together. Secondly, participants identified the CEEC support and resources as a major catalyst and facilitator of change. Besides providing the initial impetus for program evaluation, the CEEC has continued to focus attention on evaluation throughout the last 15 years. They have also provided resources and tools to support the process and institutional evaluation policy development.

Thirdly, just knowing that the CEEC will compare Dawson against other institutions serves as a strong motivator—it goes to Dawson's pride and competitive spirit. Finally, the presence of an internal, well-respected, professional evaluator (and her staff) serves as an "enabler" of a learning culture as well.

There are a number of barriers that inhibit the development of a culture of inquiry at Dawson. The most frequently mentioned barriers relate to "*resistance*" to the inquiry initiative, be it program evaluation or ongoing. Essentially, employees are comfortable in their classrooms, doing what they do best (teaching), and they may not always see the need to involve themselves in such activities. One observer remarked: "*It is a huge amount of work and it's not what they do—A teacher wants to be in the classroom teaching!*" They view evaluations as a time-consuming, bureaucratic activity (imposed by the administration), with little or no benefits. Furthermore, they feel that their workload is already heavy and the allocated release time is insufficient.

Changing the culture necessitates a new way of thinking and this is often difficult. According to one participant, "it means that they need to learn to think possibly in a different way that they aren't used to." For example, in ongoing evaluation, it is a different perspective: "We're trying to move them from their small unit to the larger institution—in a larger context." Many employees associate evaluation with fear and stress. Recent history shows that evaluations can lead to significant changes and no one wants to be involved in an evaluation that leads to cessation of a program. Accessibility of information has also been an inhibitor, "but it's one that we've recognized." Information systems are now being updated and redesigned to improve accessibility to users.

Concluding Comments

Dawson College has a considerable amount of experience with evaluation dating back to the period prior to external mandates for such information from the provincial authority. More recently, the Director General has instituted an ongoing evaluation initiative that has fuelled a good deal of inquiry within the organization.

Generally, staff at Dawson perceive that their knowledge and skill levels to conduct evaluation are low but improving. Competence tends to be built through involvement in evaluations—learning by doing. Employees rely heavily on an evaluation expert who is a source of knowledge for them. One concern is that they tend to see low learning transfer in doing evaluation, seeming to start from scratch with each new evaluation project. When doing evaluations they follow a structured process, but usually it is tailored to the specific issues of the program being evaluated. There tends to be fairly high involvement of stakeholders in evaluations, which is consistent with the ongoing evaluation initiative as well.

Dawson College staff also has the opinion that the credibility of the evaluation is important and is well ensured by a thorough vetting process with the presence of a professional evaluator and other key stakeholders, and by multiple sources of data and evidence-based recommendations. Lastly, staff see that evaluation is taken seriously and that results do have an impact and are used for change such as in program revision. They also see it as critical that there is commitment by senior management to evaluation and to building a culture of inquiry at Dawson.

CATHERINE J. ELLIOTT is an assistant professor in the Telfer School of Management at the University of Ottawa.

J. BRADLEY COUSINS is a professor of educational evaluation at the Faculty of Education and Director of the Centre for Research on Educational and Community Services (CRECS), University of Ottawa.

SWEE C. GOH is a professor emeritus in organizational behavior at the Telfer School of Management, University of Ottawa, Canada.

NEW DIRECTIONS FOR EVALUATION • DOI: 10.1002/ev

Case 2: Canadian Mental Health Association

Sarah Birnie, Tim Aubry

Introduction and Study Context

The Ottawa Branch of the Canadian Mental Health Association (CMHA) is a not-for-profit organization that has been in operation since 1953. The CMHA was created by a group of Ottawa volunteers concerned about the mental health needs of the citizens of Ottawa. The agency's objectives have largely remained the same since its inception, including social action, community service, education, and research. The agency offers a variety of services and programs that are accessible to the public as well as other organizations that support individuals within the targeted vulnerable population: individuals with severe and persistent mental illness, who experience homelessness or are at risk of becoming homeless, with co-occurring substance use disorders, who are in conflict with the law, with co-occurring developmental disability, and with other complex needs.

CMHA was noted by interviewees as being "tremendously forward thinking" and with a history of solid leadership. The culture includes an "open, facilitative model of decision making" and one that employs people who are keen to be continually changing and evolving their practice. Many in-house evaluations are conducted and the agency has consistently involved university partners over the last 15 years on larger scale projects. Although there is no specific evaluation unit at the agency, there is both upper and middle management involved in the evaluation process. All interviewees agreed that the first large-scale evaluation undertaken by the agency (with the university as a partner) was the catalyst for building evaluation capacity within the agency.

CMHA is very invested in applying for evaluation funding for each new program that is developed and is quite disappointed when the Ministry affords program funding without concomitant evaluation funding. One interviewee noted that "right from the time that we hear there is funding coming, we've already started to build an expectation for ourselves around evaluation." Another noted that "decisions about research and evaluation are made independently of the availability and/or pursuit of Ministry funding." Often, the agency applies for separate funding for evaluation projects. "We strive to go beyond merely what we are accountable for [to the Ministry]," and move toward more comprehensive evaluations that include both short- and long-term outcomes.

New Directions for Evaluation • DOI: 10.1002/ev

Drivers for Evaluation

Agency staff identified many different, but related, drivers for evaluation within the agency. Most of the comments fell within seven major categories listed below:

1. *Agency values.* CMHA is a "value-driven agency" with "very innovative thinkers who have created a culture that permits research and evaluation to thrive." Evaluation has been identified as one of the agency's five strategic directions.

2. *Determining consumer needs.* CMHA routinely uses needs assessment to determine consumer needs as well as public needs in terms of mental health education.

3. *Program monitoring.* "Is the program running the way we planned it to?" CMHA uses evaluation to monitor program implementation and to develop or validate tools that will be used for ongoing program evaluations.

4. *Outcome assessment.* Outcome assessment is the main evaluation driver identified by all interviewees for CMHA. "Are we making a difference? Are we doing the right thing? What are we learning? Are we helping clients?" The agency goes beyond the Ministry in this respect to identify and measure longer term outcomes such as functioning, attitude change, and quality of life.

5. *Contributing to the knowledge base.* Over half the interviewees noted that agency staff is committed to researching and implementing evidence-based practices and treatments within and outside the agency. According to one respondent "[Evaluation helps] us to better understand the evidence base for models so that we can better contribute to system planning that is not arbitrary but has roots in evidence."

6. *Public education and training.* The agency feels responsible for and has developed leadership in developing effective practices on a continuum of support for clients that often involve other community programs, professionals, and the public.

7. *Securing resources.* All interviewees noted that without evaluation, the agency would not have the hard evidence to present to funding bodies when seeking additional monies to implement new programs or continue to provide effective community services.

Capacity to Do Evaluation

As mentioned, there is no designated evaluation unit at CMHA, although two directors share the responsibility for overseeing evaluation projects at the agency. CMHA has a "management team that feels evaluation is a component of their everyday job" and "evaluation is a very large part of what

NEW DIRECTIONS FOR EVALUATION • DOI: 10.1002/ev

everyone does." Recently, there has been an increasing focus on involving junior managers and frontline staff involved in evaluation work. Evaluations are done either in-house or are contracted out to local university research teams depending on (a) available funds, (b) the size and scope of the evaluation, and (c) the department within the agency. Some departments, such as public education and training, simply do not have the funds to hire university teams to evaluate programs, and often do not have the human resources to devote additional time to evaluation work outside of routine pre–post workshop questionnaires.

In contrast, within the direct service provision departments, large-scale evaluations are typically contracted out, and students and professors from local universities work directly with direct service managers in planning such studies. Despite the university involvement, "on most occasions, the agency is involved in contributing significantly to the planning, data collection/analysis, and reporting process." Stakeholder involvement, perhaps with the exclusion of intended program beneficiaries, is very important in these evaluation projects and this is primarily a result of CMHA working within an integrated service delivery model. Evaluations commonly have community advisory committees comprised of consumers, family members, lawyers, mental health professionals, and an agency board member.

The CMHA personnel with the most direct contact with the university teams are in the data management area responsible for a variety of technical tasks (e.g., data entry oversight, co-coordinating data collection, liaison with management and frontline staff). Data collection efforts are often stalled due to frontline staff not completing questionnaires in a timely fashion, resulting in "baseline" data actually reflecting a client's functioning some months after their program admission. Timely communication between managers and research support team members about changes to evaluation projects was also identified as an area that could be improved. In the near future, the plan was to hire someone whose full-time job will be data management. This plan was in response to an increasing need for more sophisticated data reporting for the Ministry as well as to the increased workload of personnel with data management responsibilities.

In addition to formal evaluation studies, there were also ongoing monitoring activities conducted for the provincial Ministry of Health's data collection and monitoring system.

Evaluation Knowledge and Skill Development

With a "culture of evaluation" at CMHA, as mentioned, everyone is involved in evaluation work to some degree. Frontline staff is responsible for inputting ongoing and supplemental data on a client-by-client level. Middle management, responsible for additional data entry and analysis, puts together data for presentations given by upper management. Junior and senior managers are involved in both in-house and university-partnered evaluations at the planning stages as well as data analysis and report writing. Managers stated that if a staff member wanted to get more involved in evaluation, the opportunities would be there. However, most interviewees admitted that frontline staff struggle to keep up with data input activities given their hectic, day-to-day responsibilities. Educating staff about the importance of evaluation, informing them about results, and showing gratitude were recognized as important strategies. One senior manager noted, "You can't just slide someone an envelope and ask them to fill something out with only a sketchy explanation." Workshops and lunchtime sessions at the agency are used to help inform staff, but several interviewees noted the need for additional workshop training about basic statistics, the importance of timely and clean data, and other topics. The following comments illustrate:

> [Frontline staff] still do not know how to carry out evaluations or the importance of entering data and just see it as 'something I have to do'... you have to explain to them why you are doing the evaluation.

> [Additional] workshops would reinforce the capacity of the agency and empower people to understand the significance of [evaluation].

Two agency managers have been given the opportunity to pursue a graduate-level diploma in program evaluation with the goal of building capacity within the agency and allowing for the possibility of conducting more future in-house evaluations. According to one, this has been a "humbling exercise" as "taking the course made me appreciate the complexities in a good evaluation." The information gleaned from this certificate course has been shared with agency staff informally, as one interviewee noted that her team "does not hesitate to use internal resources [when it comes to evaluation-related questions]."

A frustration for some interviewees at the agency is the fact that funding for evaluations is typically only awarded to university research teams, and this has resulted in only limited (if any) funds for in-house evaluations at CMHA. This touched on a broader issue raised by interviewees of the "disconnect" between community agencies, hospitals, and universities, in that community research "is often an afterthought [within universities]."

Capacity to Use Evaluation

CMHA uses evaluation findings in four primary ways: securing funding, informing practice, distinguishing between different levels of outcomes at a system level, and securing ties with local universities through shared publication rights. The first is to show that their programs and treatments are evidence based as a way of securing additional Ministry funding to continue to do the work they know is helping targeted vulnerable populations. As one person put it:

NEW DIRECTIONS FOR EVALUATION • DOI: 10.1002/ev

> We didn't know how disruptive [evaluation work] was going to be, but we always knew it would be of great benefit and payoff. We knew from an academic point of view that it would contribute to our ability to do what we were doing and that then we could make claims about what we knew anecdotally [about program effectiveness].

As the following comments reveal, evaluation results are also used to shape agency practice:

> What it makes me think of is strategic planning. It makes us look at the kinds of things that we are doing and helps us identify certain issues.

> Evaluation shapes and informs our own practice.

> [Evaluation] dictates organizational and service delivery changes that are needed [within the agency].

> [Evaluation is used for] changing practice guidelines, developing new policies, and modifying programs.

Evaluation results are not only used to inform the agency of its own potential need for program changes but also as a way for the agency to know what is working and how staff are making a difference in the lives of clients. In this way, evaluation results are used in a large number of presentations each year across the country to mental health agencies, at conferences, and in workshops. This was noted by two interviewees as aiding in the "corporate branding" image of the agency and helping secure its public perception as an agency that is values driven and that promotes evaluation. Additionally, research teams from the university will often give presentations to agency staff themselves once an evaluation has terminated, as a way to "empower staff and show them they are making a difference." The upper management also noted that evaluation is used to influence decision makers in the field of mental health, and also governmental bodies in altering provincial legislation.

CMHA Ottawa has developed its capacity to distinguish between outcomes at different "system levels," in an effort to interpret evaluation findings that may be deemed a "system failure," but in actuality are successful outcomes for clients. For example, one outcome of an evaluation of service usage uptake in individuals receiving intensive case management showed that after beginning services, clients used social programs to a greater extent. Originally deemed a "system failure," as it was costing society additional funds, CMHA was able to make the case that many of these clients were underutilizing services prior to engaging in case management and many were in dire need of medical attention and social programming. Aptly put by one respondent:

As long we keep our values lens screwed on right—which is that [we are a] recovery-based and client-driven service—we won't lose track of why our outcomes might legitimately conflict with desired system outcomes.

A final way that evaluation results are used is in securing ties with university research teams. Reports are prepared in tandem with the university partners and the respondents felt that they had a strong working alliance with university evaluation team members.

Respondents also talked about process use. By being involved in the process of doing evaluation, agency staff develops skills or knowledge or experiences a change in mindset. At the managerial level, interviewees noted that evaluation involvement "enhances conscious decision making." At CMHA, management has encouraged staff at lower levels to "take ownership of small evaluation endeavors" and/or additional responsibilities in summarizing or interpreting data results. A resounding comment made about "process use" included the idea that frontline staff are challenged personally and also made to be more accountable to agency values:

It helps frontline staff remain accountable to the Agency's research goals as they are able to see the link between evaluation and accountability.

It enhances staff objectivity, flexibility, and accountability, and enables them to provide better services.

It changes staff values on a personal level such that they see the importance of evaluation beyond what is required for the Ministry.

Individuals gain insight into what they do, why they do it, and whether it works.

[You know] what is going on in the city, what the programs are, and [evaluation] keeps you informed of what is happening.

Evaluation Enablers and Barriers

Factors identified as helping to integrate evaluation into the organizational culture were primarily the commitment of upper management in making evaluation a top priority, a willingness at all levels of the agency to collect data on an ongoing basis, and when frontline staff understood the importance of evaluation and thus were accountable and committed to entering data in a timely fashion. Additional enablers were funds available for evaluation projects. As mentioned previously such resources tend to come through partnerships with universities or hospitals as a consequence of eligibility criteria.

NEW DIRECTIONS FOR EVALUATION • DOI: 10.1002/ev

All interviewees noted that the first large-scale evaluation project undertaken by CMHA in partnership with a local university was the "launching pad" for evaluation capacity building within the agency. This evaluation "shook up board members, staff, and managers" and "harnessed the momentum for that strategic direction" and was critical in securing additional program funding from the Ministry.

Evaluations that were cited as "going well" included those with concrete, specific questions, a well-honed targeted population, the use of comprehensive assessment tools, extensive stakeholder involvement as "support in doing the evaluation", and those that provided demonstrative evidence in support of the evaluated intervention. Longitudinal studies and those with a comparison group were also seen as superior. Several barriers to evaluation integration were evident as well, most notably financial and personnel resources. Frontline staff were overloaded much of the time due to the nature of working with such a vulnerable population and are often "putting out fires" during the work week, resulting in insufficient work time left to collect and enter data in a timely fashion. More than one interviewee noted that a significant barrier is the fact that the agency does not have a designated full-time position for research and evaluation.

Additional system-level barriers were identified. These included the notion that "academic institutions are required to come on board for evaluations" in order to secure financial resources from funding sources. This sentiment was nicely captured in the following quotation:

> How do you make stronger links with the university? It is also good for the university to have community links and connections. We have ideas—we'd like to do research—but we'll never get funding to do research, as you have to be associated with a university or hospital. How do you make partnerships? Honestly, that is how you are going to build capacity in the community—it's not going to happen otherwise.

This dependence on universities was viewed as a limitation to conducting many evaluations. Agency managers would like to be able to apply for evaluation funding independently, but are constrained in this respect. One interviewee noted that many university and hospital personnel do not realize the reality of practicing and doing research outside of an academic/hospital setting, and this is a limitation to securing additional partnerships with professors and/or mental health professionals who may want to partner with the agency in evaluation work. Further to this concern was the barrier identified by an interviewee of the tendency to view evaluation as merely accountability.

Several issues were raised concerning evaluations that did not go well. These included limits on the implementation of suggestions stemming from an evaluation, challenges "to find meaningful results", little to no stakeholder involvement, poor stakeholder communication, irregular data collection and entry patterns, evaluation designs with no comparison group, and participant attrition due to pre–post time lapses.

Concluding Remarks

It was obvious from the individual meetings with the interviewees that CMHA staff is very proud of their agency and the work that they do in helping such a vulnerable sector of the population of Ottawa. All interviewees noted the importance of evaluation and the agency's commitment to improving their programs and services by conducting needs assessments, implementation evaluations, and outcome evaluations. It was clear that there existed a specific series of evaluation steps driven by agency values and the quest for empirically supported treatments. CMHA is a leader in the community in terms of advocating for large-scale evaluations that are both longitudinal and utilize comparison groups, and are also committed to attempting to influence policy makers and decision makers in the community responsible for mental health legislation. Despite staff being overloaded at times and frontline staff not always understanding the importance of collecting and entering data in a timely fashion, it was clear that interviewees uniformly felt that the agency would expand exponentially in the years to come in terms of evaluation capacity through additional personnel and enhanced training of senior managers.

SARAH BIRNIE is a clinical psychologist at The Ottawa Hospital.

TIM AUBRY is a professor in the School of Psychology and codirector of the Centre for Research on Educational and Community Services at the University of Ottawa.

NEW DIRECTIONS FOR EVALUATION • DOI: 10.1002/ev

Case 3: International Development Research Centre

Courtney Amo, J. Bradley Cousins

Introduction and Study Context

The International Development Research Centre (IDRC) is an independent, Canadian crown corporation that was created by an Act of Parliament in 1970. As a donor agency, its mission of "Empowerment through Knowledge" is enacted through the support of applied research of direct benefit to developing countries and their citizens. By maintaining ongoing exchanges with its partners in developing countries, IDRC is able to support research projects in priority areas (social/economic policy; environment/national resource management; information and communication technology; innovation, policy, and science) that reflect pressing and current community needs. In addition, the Centre helps build research capacity in developing countries by providing expert advice and a significant set of resources. Secondarily, it administers special projects, and provides training support and awards for academic study and hands-on training of young researchers from Canada and developing countries.

A 21-member international Board of Governors governs the Centre. The organization reports to the Parliament of Canada through the Minister of Foreign Affairs and is not subject to the same accountability regime as other Canadian government departments and agencies. IDRC's website notes that the Centre has "been recognized by the Office of the Auditor General as a model of good corporate governance."

The Centre has six regional offices around the world (Dakar, Nairobi, Cairo, New Delhi, Singapore, and Montevideo) and organizational partnerships have been an important part of its mandate since inception. IDRC engages in three types of partnerships (hands-on research, joint funding/activity, and collaborative research) with like-minded donors, development agencies, and research institutions.

A formal evaluation function housed within the President's Office has been in place since 1991 and, at the time of the case study, was made up of 6.5 professional staff. The Unit contributes to the Centre's ability to manage risks and account for public funds by supporting the generation of evaluative evidence on the performance of the organization. At the same time, the Unit houses its own research support function aimed at addressing knowledge gaps in the area of development research evaluation. Mirroring the Centre's mission, the Unit supports Centre management to make use of evaluation in program planning and decision making by fostering a culture of organizational learning. It engaged in four broad categories of activity:

NEW DIRECTIONS FOR EVALUATION • DOI: 10.1002/ev

- conducting and disseminating strategic evaluations;
- carrying out capacity development in evaluation and evaluative thinking;
- engaging in methodology development and tools for evaluation research and evaluation; and
- developing and implementing organizational learning processes.

The Centre's evaluation mechanisms are overseen by the Evaluation Unit which is responsible for ensuring the integrity of the system and assessing the quality of evaluations against internationally accepted professional standards.

IDRC is an organization that values collaboration, consultation, and the professional and intellectual contributions of its staff members. It values the creation of specific spaces for reflection and sharing (e.g., Annual Learning Forum, staff performance reviews), and is seen by interviewees as being characterized by relatively informal communication among staff members, unhindered by hierarchy. At the same time, the diversity of the Centre's program portfolio and the challenging nature of the work can lead to the development of program-area silos—resulting in program staff not necessarily being aware of what is being done in other areas. The evaluation approach adopted by IDRC has built-in processes that make evaluation a natural mechanism for breaking down these barriers. As one interviewee puts it "one of the roles that evaluation has often [played] has been the cross-fertilization of ideas from one program area to another . . . [evaluation has played this role] sometimes quite consciously."

Drivers for Evaluation

IDRC's evaluation strategy for 2005–2010 outlines three roles for evaluation: (a) contributing to the organization's ability to account for its performance in managing public funds and demonstrate the results of its investments, (b) fulfilling the need for specialized evaluation tools and methods in the field of development research and evaluation, and (c) supporting a learning culture across the organization. "We are a research-based organization, so it is full of people whose business is inquiry. We are curiosity driven, and we have lots of people who are trained in the art of inquiry."

At the same time, interviewees noted the existence of strong evaluation champions who have and continue to strongly promote the value and use of evaluation as being an important driver for evaluation at IDRC. They also equate the use of evaluation with the evaluation approach adopted by the organization—as one interviewee puts it, "the system that has been built up not only encourages use, but almost demands use, so it's not a system that was developed to do evaluation just for evaluation's sake."

Given its reporting structure, evaluation is driven less by requirements and more by its integration into the organization's learning culture. As one respondent noted, "we don't have to participate in the ritual." As such,

IDRC's Evaluation and Results Reporting System, which was tailored to meet the organization's needs, allows for a balance between the drivers of accountability and risk management, and those of learning and continuous improvement. At the same time, interviewees noted that IDRC's continued ability to sustain this balance and develop/implement tailored monitoring and evaluation approaches is supported by its reputation for doing these things well, by the organization's desire to build its capacity for continuous improvement through inquiry and reflection, and its willingness to question whether the kinds of monitoring and evaluation activities undertaken at IDRC meet the organization's concerns for accountability.

Capacity to Do Evaluation

In support of the organization's decentralized evaluation function, the Evaluation Unit provides central coordination and technical support to program staff and management, who are ultimately responsible for their own evaluations. Each member of the evaluation team is linked to a specific program unit in order to build the Unit's understanding of, and sensitivity to, program contexts and to provide programs with a single point of contact within the Evaluation Unit.

In 2005, the Evaluation Unit underwent its first external review, which helped to develop a five-year strategy. The organization as a whole has adopted the following guiding principles for evaluation:

- Evaluations should enlist the participation of relevant users.
- Evaluation processes should develop capacity in evaluative thinking and evaluation use.
- Evaluative thinking adds value from the outset of a project or program.
- Evaluation should meet standards for ethical research and evaluation.
- The decision to evaluate should be strategic not routine.
- Evaluation should be an asset for those being evaluated.

No standardized process for conducting evaluations at IDRC exists, but there is a general reliance on a utilization-focused evaluation approach that emphasizes context appropriateness. However, there are some commonalities in the way the different types of evaluations are undertaken (e.g., problem scoping, user group development, terms of reference development, use of consultants, field work, and dissemination). Evaluations are not expected to contain recommendations; they are seen as fodder for learning, discussion, and debate. While there is no formal requirement for management responses to evaluation, there exists an expectation that programs will respond to evaluation findings and issues raised through evaluations as part of ongoing program implementation and the renewal of program initiatives.

In some cases, program staff are involved directly in the conduct of formative evaluations of programs and in many cases, evaluations actively engage senior managers. External stakeholders appear to be more regularly involved in providing data, feedback, and validation rather than conducting the evaluation. By building ownership of evaluation among user groups, the Evaluation Unit strives to strengthen IDRC's culture of evaluative thinking.

Most evaluation work at IDRC is done by external contractors and significant effort is put into developing the terms of reference and workplans for evaluation studies—often with the assistance of the Evaluation Unit. The Unit also provides assistance in the challenging task of finding the best person or people for the job. Some respondents noted the high reliance on external consultants as being a barrier to sustaining the Unit's capacity to do evaluation:

> I think there are some issues around the extent to which the people in the Evaluation Unit can be involved in doing evaluations as opposed to commenting to others and developing tools and methods. I think probably now it would be good to put a little more weight on getting our evaluation specialists involved directly in some of the evaluations.

As a monitoring mechanism IDRC developed a Rolling Project Completion Report (rPCR) process to be completed by responsible project officers through interviews conducted at three stages of a project. The interviews build on each other and provide an opportunity for probing, reflection, and sharing between the responsible officer and other members of their team. Interviewees who mentioned the rPCRs were unanimous in stating the value-added in fostering organizational learning and generating a rich data set on lessons learned and results, which would otherwise remain in the tacit knowledge base of individuals.

Overall, interviewees noted a varied level of knowledge and skills across the board. Interviewees noted that management and staff have a well-developed sense of what accounts for a good (or bad) evaluation, and there is little tolerance for low-quality evaluations. The Evaluation Unit—which is made up of individuals who hold (or are working toward) graduate degrees—was deemed by respondents to be highly skilled and knowledgeable, with the understandable exception of new staff members. Respondents noted the high level of ability of the Evaluation Unit to oversee evaluation and to ensure quality control over IDRC evaluation.

Sources of Evaluation Knowledge

Although the level of evaluation knowledge and skills of nonevaluation staff was deemed to be varied, many felt that the efforts of the Evaluation Unit in developing tools and methods, providing training and mentoring, and being an in-house resource had helped to create a higher level of evaluation knowledge and skills than could be seen in other organizations. In addition, some of IDRC's professional staff members come to the Centre with previous evaluation experiences, and, given their strong research background, most have a natural tendency toward understanding evaluation.

The Evaluation Unit's mandate of building capacity in evaluation and evaluative thinking applied both within the Centre and to IDRC partners in the field. As such, the Evaluation Unit and other Centre staff host monitoring and evaluation workshops with Centre projects in all regions:

> ...another job of the evaluation unit is really to be of assistance to improving the capacity of evaluators in different parts of the world... We think it is extremely important ... that people from the regions have an opportunity to evaluate the work that is going on in their own region...

The Evaluation Unit encourages its staff to pursue ongoing training and professional development. Sources of evaluation knowledge available to IDRC evaluation staff, program staff, management, and partners include

- advice, guidance, and mentoring through direct contact with Evaluation Unit staff;
- support in the form of a wide array of resources (e.g., learning tools, guidelines, publications, books, archives of evaluation reports);
- formal training, workshops, and exposure of staff to high-level evaluation theorists and practitioners; and
- informal training through involvement in evaluation processes.

Capacity to Use Evaluation

Explicitly acknowledged in internal policy documents are a number of uses for evaluation results and findings (e.g., decision making, improved programming, resource allocation decisions, planning, accountability, communication, learning) by a number of users (e.g., Board of Governors, Senior Management Committee, Programs, Projects). Program initiatives are expected to respond to issues raised through external reviews in their next prospectus, and the findings of these evaluations are discussed at the most senior levels of the organization. Clearly, the organization values evidence and puts a lot of weight on the intellectual rigor and scrutiny of its highly educated workforce:

> Evidence is really important. Evidence could be science or could be politics. It does not go down well to have what are seen as arbitrary decisions. ... If we understand the reasons for something, then we engage and align ourselves more readily with it. ... It needs to be seen as fair, and it needs to be seen as rational.

NEW DIRECTIONS FOR EVALUATION • DOI: 10.1002/ev

Interviewees emphasized the fact that IDRC has strived to find a balance between use of evaluation for learning and accountability purposes, with one respondent noting in particular the fact that evaluation is but one source of information available to managers. However, as noted above, this information is highly valued:

> That's why I think the overbalance for many years on the learning side was an excellent investment. In other words, the reason why we were doing evaluation was to learn and improve our own work.... It's very different if you approach things with a genuine desire to improve programs versus if you feel you have to do it...

A few respondents gave the example of these activities being used to reflect, periodically and systematically, on program and strategic directions. In particular, the rPCR process was seen as "a very powerful way of embedding reflection and diffusing knowledge within the program area ... it allows you to go in-depth into a project in a way that no other process does." In addition, the mid-term evaluations of program initiatives were seen as an opportunity to consider changes in direction—"we don't have to keep marching along." Complementing the rPCR, the Annual Learning Forum (ALF) at IDRC is a yearly event that brings together Centre staff and management from all branches for a day of learning and reflecting. As one respondent indicated

> it's an opportunity to reflect on what is being learned from evaluations rather than to build capacity in carrying out evaluation—it helps to build capacity in evaluative thinking, in [understanding] what evaluations can do for us.

Although respondents did not provide examples of political or persuasive uses of evaluation, one respondent did note that evaluations are sometimes used for symbolic purposes (e.g., evaluations of joint programming), and another noted the tendency for some studies to focus on success; he felt there is as much to learn from failures as there is from successes.

Beyond the use of evidence, interviewees saw the evaluation process as a capacity-building mechanism, and a forum for reflection and learning. As such, the benefits that emerge from involvement in, or proximity to, evaluation processes are quite present at IDRC, and respondents are well aware of them. Benefits highlighted by interviewees include

- learning about the organization, about the program, its risks, about what works and doesn't work—increased cross-fertilization of lessons and experiences (this applies to IDRC staff, management, and partners);
- learning about the context in which partners operate; greater understanding of different perspectives;

- developing a common, more sophisticated language around substantive issues as well as monitoring and evaluation;
- developing monitoring and evaluation skills and transferring this to other tasks such as program design and development; understanding evaluation as a tool for accountability and learning; and
- legitimizing and/or valuing of certain results (e.g., value of spending time building relationships); increased ability to recognize accomplishments and devise ways to move forward.

Evaluation Enablers and Barriers

IDRC is a learning organization and cultural disposition has served as an enabler for evaluation. Almost a decade ago, senior management asked itself hard questions about evaluation:

> we decided to look at about 60 evaluations in one go over a couple of days, and I think frankly we were shocked ... we were shocked at either how useless a lot of them were because in fact, things had been evaluated, there wasn't even a program anymore—doing ritualistic evaluation, really not helpful.

This was identified as a pivotal point that has led to evaluation being "part of the fabric of the organization."

Interviewees noted a number of other factors and forces that have helped to integrate evaluation into the organizational culture. These are listed below and occur at the level of the organization, of its systems, and at the level of individuals operating within the system. In addition, the utilization-focused evaluation approach adopted by IDRC is seen as an important factor in explaining the organization's capacity to do and to use evaluation:

- *Organizational factors.* Status as a crown corporation; culture of learning; valuing of evaluation at the level of the Board of Governors and Senior Management; stability of environment, of organization's budget; clarity of expression of information needs; and the favorable profile of evaluation within and outside the organization.
- *Systems/mechanisms.* Strong evaluation system and infrastructure that ensures things get done; connections between program people and Evaluation Unit; staff incentives.
- *People.* Strong level of research and/or evaluation capacity throughout the organization; leadership taking evaluation seriously; Evaluation Unit staff.
- *Evaluation approach.* Conscious learning/accountability; developing culture of evaluative thinking; innovative evaluation methodologies; evaluation approach that mirrors the organization's culture of consultation,

collaboration, stakeholder participation, and that has built-in opportunities to stop and reflect.

Although all signs point to an organization with very high evaluation capacity, interviewees raised a few points that may impede on the organization's ability to maintain and increase this capacity. For instance, one respondent noted that the organization has been successful in establishing a number of important financial partnerships that bring with them specific evaluation, monitoring, and accountability requirements, which are not always aligned with the Centre's culture. Adaptation to such circumstances was seen as being a challenge for the future.

Some interviewees noted the challenge of balancing workload against the benefits of involvement in monitoring and evaluation processes. As one respondent put it (with respect to rPCRs): "people say that we can't keep up with it. People know that there are benefits from the process but it has been identified for adding too much workload."

Other barriers are noted below and, again, can be seen to occur at the level of the organization, of its systems, and of individuals:

- *Organizational factors.* Growth in the size of programming and resulting pressure on all to do more; communication barriers between staff and management hindering the circulation of ideas.
- *Systems/mechanisms.* Tension between time/resources spent granting versus learning/reflection.
- *People.* People who don't see the value of evaluation, or who have a reductionist view of the purpose of evaluation; perhaps too much stability in staff complement.
- *Evaluation approach/products.* Limits on diversity of methods, potential influence of evaluation trends and fashions; occasional generation of low-quality evaluation or poorly done evaluation.
- *External concerns.* Federal government emphasis on accountability; demand for scarce evaluation resources in developing countries; and shortage of expertise and skills in consulting community.

Concluding Comments

IDRC's high level of capacity to *do* and to *use* evaluation can be attributed to a number of factors that relate to the organization, its systems, its staff, and the approach it has adopted for evaluation. Most important in the minds of those interviewed is the fact that IDRC is a research-based organization, that evaluation has the support of the highest levels of the organization, and that the Centre (and the Evaluation Unit) has spent many years cultivating a balance between evaluation for learning and evaluation for accountability. In addition, the numerous benefits that have emerged from evaluation findings and involvement in evaluation processes contribute to the reinforcement of the value of monitoring and evaluation activities, despite the time and effort these require.

Although it was noted that evaluation capacity cannot blossom in a hostile operating environment, one nonevaluator respondent speculated whether evaluation capacity could have a protective effect on an organization—whether an organization with high evaluation capacity would be in a better position to defend, justify itself, should cuts happen. This respondent also asked what would be the impact of not having a high level of evaluation capacity, and when, in the life of an organization, does reflection become necessary and value-added. Such questions give insight into an organization where the level of reflection on evaluation is quite sophisticated.

COURTNEY AMO is Manager, Evaluation, at the Atlantic Canada Opportunities Agency, Moncton, New Brunswick, Canada.

J. BRADLEY COUSINS is a professor of educational evaluation at the Faculty of Education and Director of the Centre for Research on Educational and Community Services (CRECS), University of Ottawa.

NEW DIRECTIONS FOR EVALUATION • DOI: 10.1002/ev

Case 4: Canadian Cancer Society

Steve Montague, Anne Vezina, Sharon Campbell, Anna Engman

Introduction and Study Context

The CCS, founded in 1938, is the largest health charity in Canada. It raises in excess of $180 million per year through various fundraising activities and special events. The funds are spent on research, information, prevention, advocacy, and support services targeted to the reduction of incidence and mortality rates due to cancer and the enhancement of the quality of life of those living with cancer. The organization receives almost all of its funds from donations. The organization's mission is pursued through the work of committed volunteers and staff. Across the country the CCS has approximately 1,200 employees and close to 170,000 volunteers. Leadership is shared between the National Board of Directors and 10 Division Boards of volunteers working with their respective Executive Directors/CEOs.

The 10 Division Executive Directors/CEOs and the National CEO form the Executive Leadership Team (ELT) which is responsible for the strategic leadership of the organization. In the early 2000s, ELT recognized the importance of performance management to monitor and measure progress toward identified goals and in 2006 established the Performance Management Team (PMT). The mandate of the group is not explicitly to promote evaluation capacity per se, but its role in building internal capacity for performance management and in monitoring and reporting nationwide progress requires evaluation. While its mandate did incorporate improved performance monitoring, reporting, and management—as well as accountability—the term "evaluation" was not explicitly stated or defined. Even though the CCS still does not have a national evaluation plan, it has recently recognized the need for one as a result of its first nationwide report on performance.

The CCS does not have an internal team dedicated to evaluation. Instead, the CCS created the Center for Behavioral Research and Program Evaluation (CBRPE) in 1993 through its research partner the National Cancer Institute of Canada (NCIC).[4] The CCS was responding to the need for more behavioral cancer research in Canada and the increased focus on accountability in the not-for-profit sector (Broadbent, 1999). The creation of CBRPE and subsequent close working relationship between CBRPE and the CCS started to build an awareness of the importance and benefits of evaluation as a corporate capacity.

Based at the University of Waterloo, CBRPE's original objectives were to build the field of social and behavioral cancer research in Canada, create

NEW DIRECTIONS FOR EVALUATION • DOI: 10.1002/ev

a pan-Canadian sociobehavioral cancer research network, and enhance CCS capacity for using evaluation and research evidence in guiding decision making. With annual core funding of $2.6 million, CBRPE supports a sociobehavioral research network across Canada, a professional Evaluation Studies Unit (ESU), and five scientists who conduct population-based evaluation and research studies.

There are many user groups for evaluation in the CCS. They include directors of national and division programs and national office directors. The programs delivered by the CCS from coast to coast (e.g., Cancer Information Service, Peer Support, Relay for Life, and Smokers' Helpline) undergo both continuous quality improvement studies and periodic outcome studies. Evaluative studies of provincially based programs range from basic surveys to more fulsome evaluation designs. Functional groups such as marketing, revenue development, and communications may also conduct evaluations, either to help plan new initiatives, or to assess existing campaigns. Nationwide public opinion research is used to understand perception of Canadians toward the CCS brand, level of awareness of its health messages, programs, and services, and attitude toward giving.

Drivers for Evaluation

We identified three key drivers for evaluation at the CCS. The first driver is accountability to Canadians and donors who are represented by national and divisional boards. In the charitable health sector, reduction in disease incidence and the improvement of the quality of life of cancer patients is difficult to attribute to one organization only. The lack of easily attributable outcome results for most CCS mission initiatives intensifies the need for better performance management monitoring reports with evidence to demonstrate progress toward the "Ends," a series of formal organizational objectives.

The second driver relates to learning and improvement. The CCS engages highly motivated staff and volunteers who want to know what difference they make and want to improve performance wherever they can. It has a stated intent to become a learning organization and offers many opportunities for professional development for staff and volunteers. Managers, senior executives, and board members all recognized this goal—and further noted some early progress. In the words of one manager "We are a highly distributed organization across the country so it is impossible to move everybody in the same direction at the same time at the same pace"; on the other hand, in the words of one member of senior leadership "I think we have made a lot of progress in clarifying the different levels of planning and evaluation and how they relate to each other. We get better and better at integrating strategic goals into individual performance plans."

Despite the many changes underway and the successes in building CCS' capacity for evaluation, according to one interviewee, one of the recognized limitations of the past evaluation structure has been "that evaluations have … been ad-hoc. CBRPE only does what people ask them to do. … a more robust framework for evaluation [is needed]." But challenges in getting there remain. Barriers such as size and diversity were noted by some respondents: one interviewee characterized the CCS as a "dancing elephant." Others noted barriers such as a lack of tolerance for mistakes, sometimes being too nice to focus on individual improvements and sometimes being unwilling to really strive for improvement. Two interviewees specifically noted the need to promote better sharing of evaluation and evaluative information as a means for improvement.

The third driver that we identified is the close relationship between CCS and its research partner, the National Cancer Institute of Canada (NCIC). The CCS and NCIC share a CEO, and each CCS Division allocates a significant proportion of its revenue to the NCIC to support its research agenda. The NCIC has an international peer review panel and funds research across the cancer continuum. This proximity to a research organization with the same CEO has led to an awareness and commitment to the use of evidence in CCS decision making.

Capacity to Do Evaluation

CCS' capacity for evaluation greatly depends on its relationship with CBRPE. The ESU helps CCS monitor alignment and progress toward objectives, and provides key indicators and evaluation findings to support performance management, planning, and budget allocation. CBRPE also conducts specific evaluations of CCS services and programs; undertakes literature reviews, knowledge synthesis, and best practice assessments; develops instruments and data collection protocols for CCS to use with its own evaluations; and provides scientific analysis of CCS data. In addition, ESU is engaged both formally and informally in advisory roles to CCS program directors.

In the last 10 years, CBRPE's expertise in behavioral and social science has influenced and transferred knowledge to the various staff and volunteers across the organization in areas such as social marketing, communications, public health promotion, service quality assurance, and other key CCS initiatives. Evaluation capacity within CCS has been built by deliberately engaging staff on all levels of an evaluation project. In the words of one member of senior leadership "The divisions always participate on the working committees/teams."

Over time, the CCS has increasingly developed its evaluation expertise with a cadre of both staff and core consultants across the country. This resource has started to demonstrate its potential when focused on key program areas (e.g., Tobacco Control, Cancer Information Service, and Cancer Connection). Staff has developed an understanding of the key elements of evaluation to work with CBRPE to design questionnaires, recruitment methodologies, and data analysis frameworks that lead to relevant and scientifically sound results. It is notable that recent evaluation studies have had wide CCS engagement in discussions of appropriate sampling and instrument design (e.g., Cancer Connection and Cancer Information Service evaluations).

Senior staff statements support the notion that—while CBRPE plays the role as leading technical expert—CCS managers are often actively involved in evaluation studies: "Staff provides feedback on evaluation design and have influence over the type of questions that are asked in the evaluation. Staff are both involved in drafting and approving feedback on interview guides. Staff are engaged on all levels."

The process of evaluative inquiry has taken different paths within the organization. A systematic evaluation process is used for core programs in the form of client surveys to assess the level of satisfaction using the Larsen scale (Larsen, Attkinson, Hargreaves, & Nguyen, 1979) and to assess the impact of the programs in improving knowledge, attitudes, and behaviors. For example, both information and support programs employ anonymous mailed surveys to monitor client satisfaction on a continuous basis, with periodic telephone surveys of a random sample of clients to assess whether these programs helped clients better understand and cope with their cancer, take actions toward prevention (if applicable), or support families or friends with cancer. Evaluations of functional areas such as fundraising campaigns (e.g., Relay for Life) examine differences between high and low revenue generating events. A cost-benefit evaluation of telephone "quitlines" was used to support continued government funding. Other evaluation cases specific to Divisions vary in terms of the inquiry process used, based on each Division's specific needs and protocols.

Capacity to Use Evaluation

The CCS has many users for evaluation and as such displays a variety of perceptions of the function. As noted above, evaluation is used for both accountability and for learning/service delivery improvement. Furthermore, due to the progressive integration of evaluation into performance reporting at national and divisional levels, evaluation is sometimes blurred with the concept of monitoring. Some small evaluative studies would be better considered in the vein of monitoring reports than in the category of evaluation. Indeed, data on program utilization, reach, and outcomes for some of these programs are now routinely incorporated into the National Board Ends Report.

In the years prior to 2008, the nationwide Performance Management Team (PMT) started to incorporate evaluative thinking into the organization's definition of its mission, its planning, progress measurement, and reporting functions—ultimately influencing changes in strategic directions and priorities. In this way, evaluation is not perceived as a distinct function in and of itself but rather an essential tool for aligning resources to impact at various levels. Evidence-based discussions on progress and impact of the CCS's initiatives, programs, and services are increasingly taking place at board and senior staff levels. In part, this can be attributed to the idea of a "results chain."

The new focus on performance management implies a mandate to build capacity to use evaluation findings. In this way, the PMT is gathering evaluative information, increasing the organization's ability to interpret results and to understand the implications for better alignment of resources to outcomes. It is also helping to organize evaluative knowledge systems, thereby building evaluative information and knowledge capacity. The PMT is increasingly seen as a source of performance management expertise for planning, measuring/monitoring, reporting, and managing. It is promoting learning and knowledge transfer within the organization. Furthermore, it is serving the three functions of facilitating evaluative activities, facilitating evaluative learning, and creating evaluative information—as outlined by Mayne and Rist (2006) and described in more detail below.

Facilitating Evaluative Activities

The first task for the PMT was to consolidate the thinking from previous evaluation work and divisional balanced scorecard work into one framework for the CCS. Over the course of three years, the organization developed and honed what became known as a results chain or hierarchy as a framework for designing services, programs, and policies to achieve results. This hierarchy was first used to help focus the overall CCS mission and targets. The mission was rearticulated taking six priorities—and 34 "results statements"—and organizing them under two key "mega" ends (reduction of incidence of cancer and enhancement of quality of life), four subends, and two organizational means that serve as the overall vision for the organization.

In parallel with this work the PMT used the results hierarchy to reconcile and integrate divisions using the balanced scorecard with divisions using other performance management systems. This resulted in a retrospective recasting of performance information into a results hierarchy structure that summarized the performance of each division and the national organization as part of an overall performance report for the organization. The synthesis resulted in a more concise report illustrating in a results chain format the relationships between inputs/outputs of programs and initiatives to reach, reactions, and impact on knowledge and behaviors in target audiences (general public, people living with cancer, policy makers, donors, volunteers, and staff). This focus on impact instead of activities has been welcomed by board members, senior staff, program staff, and volunteers as they have been exposed to the concepts and approach.

In the words of one senior leader: "A common language and common framework has been a key foundation. What helped was that the model was logical. It made sense to people regardless of area. They could see their work feed into it." However, the exercise has also revealed gaps. A number of respondents noted the fact that the "sorting" of evidence by the results chain was important because it showed gaps as well as progress.

Facilitating Evaluative Learning

Three summit sessions were held with key managers in order to engage them in the development of a results framework based on the organizational "Ends." Following these sessions, three regional education sessions were held. The sessions had two objectives. The first was to validate the revised and streamlined mission map and the second was to learn about and develop hands-on knowledge of the results framework. This training trend continued throughout the year with one- or two-day divisional training sessions involving both staff and board members. In this way, evaluative capacity is built in conceptual and process use terms first—*then* used as context for direct strategic, tactical, and operational uses.

Creating Evaluative Information

The CBRPE is a member of the CCS-PMT team and acts as a vital connection to the world of research in areas of behavioral- and population-based cancer control, health promotion, prevention, community-based support, and evaluation sciences. The group is also actively involved in efforts to improve measurement of behavioral changes in target communities, such as smokers. The broader PMT is also taking steps to codify, formalize, and share (via a web-based system) results hierarchies, data collection tools, performance information and tools, tips, and techniques.

The consolidated Ends report produced in 2007 represents the synthesis of progress from a diverse set of sources. As mentioned previously, the key to this has been the development of a common framework and a common language with which to communicate results performance. The adapted Bennett hierarchy levels that make up the results framework have served this purpose well and have started to permeate the conversations among staff, between staff and management, and even between board and staff. It has focused the discussions on how to have an impact and link resources to relevant outcomes. In one case, a board Performance Assurance Committee member asked a senior staff member to synthesize the critical elements for the business case of a new program. Using the results chain framework, she was able to identify the relevant spheres of influence and capture the desired results in one page. The response was "This is exactly what I was looking for!"

Evaluation Enablers and Barriers

Clearly, CCS' evaluation capacity has been heavily shaped and influenced by its relationship with CBRPE and the Evaluation Studies Unit and particularly from the work of the PMT. Through contributions from these units coupled with an explicit commitment by CCS to become a learning organization, an emergence of an organizational culture of evaluation is in the offing.

The "culture" of evaluation in this case is really not so much a culture of evaluation in its conventional form but rather a culture of managing for results. Within the realm of policy governance, the CCS has merged and evolved two different cultural traditions in this regard, one from the social science and health research community—steeped in traditional evaluation approaches and values—and the other from a more recent business management and balanced scorecard culture. A new mindset is emerging form the best of the two cultures.

In addition to these enablers, we observed the following:

- Strong CCS leadership and expertise.
- The application of a common results-based framework on the organization as a whole and its role in developing a common language among organization members.
- Champions of evaluation, monitoring, and evidence-based decision making on the national and local levels.

However, despite progress made in this area, the following barriers were raised by respondents:

- The size of the organization intrudes on both communication to staff and sharing of negative evaluation findings among divisions for learning purposes.
- Getting staff on board/making evaluation into a priority/making people understand what it is, what the value is, and why they are doing it (volunteers seem to present particular challenges).
- Time and resources required for making changes and reporting on an ongoing basis.
- Technical difficulties with outcome measurement.
- Results are not always directly attributable to CCS.

Concluding Comments

The CCS has displayed several elements of a new vision of evaluative capacity for organizations. The organization has assigned a transitional team, with wide participation and strong senior leadership, to help the organization to first conceptually understand evaluative thinking—specifically the results chain or logic—then to apply it to its own established performance reporting requirements, planning, and management processes. Evaluation is playing a critical part in a process of integrating evaluation into the organizational culture. While the organization is only beginning to realize its vision and potential as a fully integrated, results-oriented organization, it is living proof that evaluative thinking and capacity can quickly emerge to directly assist conventional management functions and institutions.

The CCS has grown its evaluation capacity through creation of the CBRPE with a specific mandate to work with CCS to enhance evaluative knowledge, skills, and capacity. CCS is choosing to integrate evaluation with its performance management initiative and continue its close linkages with CBRPE. Time will tell whether this approach will strengthen the function by directly tying it to mainstream corporate functions, or whether it will be weakened by being subsumed into other functions (e.g., ongoing monitoring and measures development for planning). So far, the use of a results chain as a key organizing principle—along with the solid and consistent work of CBPRE—has preserved evaluation as a distinct and valued function in the organization. The Mayne–Rist hypothesis—that in order to thrive (and possibly even to survive) evaluation must directly serve core policy and management functions—would appear to be validated in this case.

STEVE MONTAGUE *is a career evaluation practitioner, partner at Performance Management Network Inc., adjunct professor at Carleton University, and fellow of the Canadian Evaluation Society.*

ANNE VEZINA *is former vice president, Strategy Performance for the Canadian Cancer Society, where she served as acting president and CEO at the time of the study.*

SHARON CAMPBELL *is a senior scientist at the Propel Centre for Population Health Impact and research associate professor in applied health sciences at the School of Public Health and Health Systems, University of Waterloo, Waterloo, Ontario, Canada.*

ANNA ENGMAN *is a senior program evaluation officer at the Natural Sciences and Engineering Research Council of Canada and the Social Sciences and Humanities Research Council of Canada.*

NEW DIRECTIONS FOR EVALUATION • DOI: 10.1002/ev

Case 5: Canada Revenue Agency

Swee C. Goh, Catherine J. Elliott

Introduction and Study Context

The Canada Revenue Agency (CRA) is a large federal government agency responsible for administering tax laws for most provinces and territories as well as benefits and incentive programs delivered through the tax system. As a typical federal government department, headquarters are located in Ottawa, but it also has large regional offices and tax centers in major urban areas. It has a functional organization structure with groupings such as appeals, collections, finance and administration, compliance programs, assessment and benefits, technology, human resources, and audit and evaluation. One of the major activities is the processing of tax returns from individual Canadians and corporations.

At the head of the organization is the Commissioner who is the chief executive officer of the agency and responsible for the day-to-day management of the organization. There is also a Board of Management, comprised of 15 people, responsible for overseeing the organization and administration of the agency and the management of its resources, services, property, personnel, and contracts. Consistent with global trends in public sector governance, CRA's evaluation function has recently moved from an operational perspective to a results-based perspective. This has required a considerable amount of reform and capacity building and represents a significant challenge for the agency.

Under the Director-General (DG) of Audit and Evaluation is a group of auditors and evaluators who perform their duties internally at CRA. They are separated into two groups each under a director. The DG reports directly to the Commissioner. The work of the auditors and the evaluators generally does not overlap but there are some instances when evaluation and audit may be performing work in the same area; as well, there is a general perception among both evaluators and users alike that the distinction between evaluation and audit is sometimes a bit "blurry" and not clearly understood.

CRA in general tends to be top down in decision making and driven by governance procedures and policy. As in most organizations of this size, communication tends to be somewhat bureaucratic; and sometimes messages may get lost, slowed down, or do not reach the intended recipients (e.g., those in the field or at lower levels). This can result in somewhat of a disconnect. In general, the participants felt that communication within their function was fairly good and within the larger agency they recognized the need for improvement, but also the challenge of striking the appropriate

NEW DIRECTIONS FOR EVALUATION • DOI: 10.1002/ev

balance between the right type of information and the right volume (i.e., what they truly "need to know"). As one senior manager remarked, "We are pretty good at coordinating things, given the size of the organization."

Drivers for Evaluation

Study participants had different views about what are the principal drivers for evaluation at CRA. Some saw evaluation to be motivated by the Director and DG after consultations with the Assistant Commissioners. However, sometimes demand comes directly from the Commissioner or the Resource Investment Management Committee (RIMC). Political pressures or a perceived problem in the Agency were identified to be forces driving evaluation as well. The evaluation unit is sometimes required to respond to the immediate needs of the Agency Management Committee or the Commissioner, if they are asked to evaluate a particular program or activity of concern.

Program evaluation has had a somewhat varied history at CRA. Participants described how the program evaluation group has experienced periodic ups and downs in terms of its impact, its reputation, and visibility. There was a period of time when very few true program evaluations were being conducted; instead, the evaluation group was doing reviews or evaluations of corporate functions. As little as four years ago, there was even a question of whether the group should exist and it had a very low profile in CRA.

However, there is a slow but growing change. Evaluation now has more support and visibility in the very senior cadre of the organization—the last two Commissioners have been very proevaluation and the DG now sits on the Agency Management Committee (AMC). This enables her to better communicate the role and contribution of evaluation at CRA, and it provides an avenue for quicker access to decision making (note: evaluation used to report through an Audit and Evaluation Committee). As one evaluator credits the DG with making significant progress: "she has been an excellent champion at the AMC." As a strong advocate of evaluation, the DG has led a strengthening initiative to demonstrate the relevance of evaluation as leverage for strategic decision making. As evidenced by one respondent's comments, many senior managers do indeed perceive evaluation as providing valuable data to inform decisions:

> To me it provides information to senior folks so that they can make decisions with their eyes wide open.

The participants felt strongly that evaluation needs to be proactive, part of the strategic priorities of the organization. For example, all new initiatives should have a sound program evaluation plan at the beginning of a new program. There needs to be a mindset among senior managers and program managers that evaluation is an integral part of any strategic program or initiative. As one person working in evaluation put it:

> We need to drive the Agency as well, especially the bigger programs, we need a cyclical review of such programs, we need to start building that in the overall agency plan and put it in the annual report.

Capacity to Do Evaluation

Currently, the Program Evaluation Division is a relatively small shop and considered to be understaffed. There is presently a staff complement of 15 employees with three Program Evaluation Managers and a Senior Advisor of Methodology reporting to the Director. Many of the evaluators are reasonably new and lack strong experience in either evaluation or in program management. Although there has been a concerted effort at recruiting new evaluators, they have been experiencing difficulty in retaining these new employees. Many reasons were cited for this high turnover (e.g., an extremely competitive environment across the federal public service, a misalignment of skills, and different generational attitude among some of the younger new hires). We had a sense from participants that some of the new recruits are highly educated and innovative but may not fully recognize or appreciate the organizational experience of others and the value that it can bring in terms of building relationships and credibility for evaluation.

The division sees itself as providing advice, feedback, and information for decision making to senior managers. Although unit members typically perform evaluations of high-priority programs, they are sometimes involved in related activities, such as developing Results-based Management and Accountability Frameworks (RMAF)[5] including indicator development for program monitoring. One unique characteristic of the group is that they do most of the evaluation themselves in-house and seldom contract out, a departure from many other departments and agencies across the Canadian federal government. Those few that are contracted out are for specific expertise or technical knowledge that is required on a project.

Most interviewees agreed that there is a conscious attempt to involve stakeholders in evaluations. The type and level of involvement range from relatively minor participation at the beginning of the evaluation (e.g., consulting program managers before the start of an evaluation) to very heavy involvement throughout the majority of data collection (e.g., actually having a subject matter expert on the team). Input on RMAFs was seen as a principal means of engaging with program decision makers and critical for furnishing knowledge or expertise about a program and augmenting the team's collective resources. This sometimes translated time to completion reduction and increased the data quality assurance. The following remarks illustrate this "valued-added" element:

NEW DIRECTIONS FOR EVALUATION • DOI: 10.1002/ev

> We get people seconded to work on this all the time. That is best because they know the programs inside out and we save so much time, especially the more complicated ones.

> Program managers are always interviewed for the [RMAF]. You go in and ask them what do they think is working well and what do you think could be improved? What would they like to see done? To get their input.

Yet it is not clear that stakeholder involvement necessarily enhanced ownership or utility of the evaluation. Frequently, there was not a full recognition (by the users) of how evaluation relates to their everyday, operational duties. Although users are well informed and consulted throughout the process, one respondent observes:

> I think that they are missing a link .... They know we are evaluation and we report to the [Assistant Commissioner], so they know how important it is that they participate in the study, but they don't see how it impacts their day to day activities.

The evaluation group presently has about 15 employees at headquarters. To supplement their evaluation team, they are sometimes able to "borrow" program personnel, as mentioned above. On occasion, they can also ask the Audit Division for assistance, particularly when auditors have specific knowledge about or experience in the programs/projects being studied. Evaluators follow a standardized process for all evaluation projects in developing frameworks, consulting clients or stakeholders, and providing feedback and reports. They do not use any fixed templates but would like to see the development of more tools and up-to-date manuals.

Sources of Evaluation Knowledge and Skills

There was a general consensus among all evaluators that the current level of evaluation knowledge within the team needs to be raised. Some challenges that were cited include: the recent retirement of experienced evaluators, the difficulty of hiring and retaining new recruits, and the lack of a standardized knowledge base and tools to support all evaluators (and particularly the new hires). Some of the newer evaluators who have joined CRA recently have been trained through courses offered by the Canadian Evaluation Society (CES) through in-house training courses or by learning on the job. Although the evaluators who were interviewed believed that new recruits could develop those core evaluation competencies (e.g., analytical skills, writing, and research skills) fairly quickly, they also felt that acquiring a solid understanding of CRA programs and the ability to deal effectively with senior managers would take a longer period of time to develop. Knowing the organization and having the skills to interact effectively with managers were seen to be as important as technical evaluation skills.

In general, there was a capacity-building challenge in terms of quickly integrating a group of new employees from outside the Corporate Audit and Evaluation Branch into a small evaluation unit comprised of very experienced evaluators. The evaluators who were interviewed felt that the challenge of integrating several new employees within a short period of time could best be dealt with by undertaking team-building activities that promote mutual understanding among members of the group. This would help to create an environment where sharing of experience and ideas takes place.

The majority of participants believed that on-the-job experience was the prime source of evaluation knowledge, but that can take a while, often more than a year to develop. Training, on the other hand, is not seen, in and of itself, to be sufficient. It is the combination of training and on-the-job experience that is seen to be the most effective. To this end, less experienced evaluators have been teamed up with those who are more experienced:

> Some of them were teamed up [with an experienced evaluator] to learn on the job. They just finished an evaluation that had to be done in 2.5 months. That was good experience because we went through all the same steps as a longer, more extensive evaluation. So they got a really compressed learning environment. That's a good way to teach them.

Capacity to Use Evaluation

There has been a lack of understanding of the benefits of evaluation—what it can do for the senior managers at CRA. The current DG is very supportive and proactive in giving more visibility to evaluation. Also, the current Commissioner has a background in evaluation that is likely to help. More recently, the evaluators feel optimistic that they have been gaining recognition for some of their "value-added" work. For example, studies such as a recent strategy for evaluating the Goods and Services Tax (GST) have been acknowledged as being highly relevant and having a significant impact on the organization. However, there was still a feeling overall that evaluation is not well understood. In the words of some of the participants:

> We need to continue to tell others about the benefits of evaluation versus audit, but there is also a reticence of senior managers to engage us at the senior level in the start of new business initiatives . . .

> . . . still there is not a lot of understanding about evaluation, it's not high profile; but this has changed, it has better profile now, better communications by the DG about what we can do . . .

There were many comments and references to the "Secure Channel" study as a recent example of an evaluation product that had a significant impact and bolstered the evaluation group's visibility at the senior level. It also demonstrated what the group can do in terms of providing good third-party information to aid in program-level decision making:

> It was used to make some strategic decisions and it was used to position the Agency to address concerns that it was facing.

Although much progress has been made, respondents felt that more needs to be done—to educate users and "sell" the value of evaluation at CRA. One suggestion was to be more proactive in engaging and consulting senior managers about critical issues—to give the group more presence and to identify where evaluation could add value early in the game. This would ensure that evaluation was linked at the front end of new projects and initiatives to ensure that funds are allocated for evaluations so that it actually happens (rather than being an expensive after thought).

Evaluation Enablers and Barriers

Overall, the capacity to use evaluation at CRA is moderate, but improving. In their responses, participants tended to be positive and forward looking about factors and forces likely to affect the integration of evaluation into the organizational culture.

To increase use, both evaluators and users felt that producing "good credible reports" and "good evidence to support our products" was essential. Reports must have solid methodology and the message and results must be seen as adding value. However, they must be timely; and they should be targeted so that only the "right ones" are performed; otherwise, they risk being perceived by senior decision makers (e.g., Assistant Commissioners) as "irrelevant," not "useful," or a "nuisance." Furthermore, one decision maker suggested that, by being more "agile," evaluation use would increase, as resources could be shifted toward those issues/projects that are highest in need. This same person recommended a "midpoint check" of all evaluations to ensure that they are still "doable" or "useable." If not, resources could be shifted.

Another aspect that was seen as important in encouraging use is consistent and rigorous follow-up. Oftentimes, there is a fair amount of attention on the evaluation report itself, but little continued interest after it is complete. Sometimes, as one evaluator commented, "things tend to fall by the wayside after we present it." In fact, many of the evaluators noted that they are not sure what happens to their recommendations afterward—or the action plans that are formulated by the branches. Several noted that it depends on the nature of the study and the degree of commitment by senior management. They felt that senior managers need to be seen as being on board and they must demonstrate their commitment to the process, the results, and the value of evaluation in order to facilitate utilization. But, overall, the support of the Commissioner, which was the case at the time, was seen to be the most important factor in terms of encouraging use. Another comment was that evaluations need to be proactive and better aligned to the strategic priorities and business plan of the department. This means that evaluation needs to be integrally involved in the Agency planning process by reviewing the bigger program areas (during the annual planning process program managers will often identify small issues that aren't strategic). How data are presented in reports is also important. For example, evaluators need to find a concise, user-friendly way of presenting credible data to support important conclusions; sometimes, there is "too much that says nothing and not too much that says something." Evaluators have been known, in the past, for preparing lengthy, difficult-to-read "tomes" of information. To encourage use, succinct, evidence-based reports are needed.

Evaluators also felt strongly that their program managers need to be educated on their role and the added value that evaluators and evaluations can bring to their programs. For example, some may be unaware of the range of evaluators' expertise. They may not know that evaluators can also assist them in performance measurement, defining outcomes, and developing RMAF's. Several evaluators suggested that they could be more proactive in approaching program managers and assessing their measurement needs; in this way, they could determine how best to assist them. A good starting point for building credibility and understanding is to help program managers experience success with an evaluation. In this way, evaluation would be more likely to connect with ongoing priorities within the Agency:

> The program managers, (from what I've seen), don't seem to understand the role that we play ... The ability to use it probably could be better.

> Evaluators need to build bridges to be useful. As long as the evaluators build bridges well, they will be useful.

Concluding Comments

The evaluation group at CRA is relatively small and growing slowly but has not yet reached its full potential. Issues around hiring and retention of new evaluators and the retirement of experienced evaluators is an ongoing challenge. The DG is seen to be a strong advocate and champion of evaluation at CRA; as a member of the AMC, she has direct access to the senior management team and is successfully raising the profile of evaluation and educating the senior management team about its crucial role—to provide objective, third-party information for decision making (and independent oversight—that is different than internal audit). The new Commissioner is also seen to be proevaluation that bodes well for future success.

At the time, the evaluation team was very much focused on building their capacity to do evaluation (some training and much learning by doing), although organization members acknowledged the need for growth in the Agency's capacity to use it. There is a widespread perception among evaluators that evaluation continues to be not well understood by senior managers and program managers. There was a persistent confusion between audit and evaluation—what is the difference, what is their value proposition, and why are they sometimes investigating the same programs? There was a general sense that by building bridges and experiencing success with evaluation, program managers can learn firsthand about the benefits of evaluation for their programs. By producing timely, relevant and credible evaluations that are directly linked to the strategic imperatives of the Agency, senior managers were expected to increasingly begin to recognize the value evaluation has to offer.

SWEE C. GOH is a professor emeritus in organizational behavior at the Telfer School of Management, University of Ottawa, Canada.

CATHERINE J. ELLIOTT is an assistant professor in the Telfer School of Management at the University of Ottawa.

NEW DIRECTIONS FOR EVALUATION • DOI: 10.1002/ev

Case 6: Human Resources and Skills Development Canada

Isabelle Bourgeois, Robert E. Lahey

Introduction and Study Context

Human Resources and Skills Development Canada (HRSDC) is one of the largest federal departments in Canada, responsible for a variety of both labor market programs (job creation, counseling, etc.) and social programs aimed at a variety of beneficiaries. Many of its programs feature grants and contributions provided by the department to third-party organizations responsible for the creation and development of specific interventions. Additionally, the organization has significant engagement with the provinces, territories, and national Aboriginal organizations. Its programs have high visibility, both publicly and politically.

Among all Canadian federal government departments, it probably has the longest history of formalized evaluation (over 30 years), and also has the largest internal evaluation unit of all departments and agencies. It has been officially recognized by Treasury Board Secretariat (TBS) for its exemplary work in the field of evaluation, and thus can yield useful ideas for organizations interested in improving their own evaluation capacity.

The Evaluation Directorate is headed by a Director General responsible for five separate units, each representing a different focus and different client base, including program areas, special initiatives, and knowledge management. The Evaluation Directorate employs 55 Full-Time Equivalents (FTEs) with a resource budget of $12 million ($8 million for operations and management and $4 million for salaries). Organizationally, the Evaluation Directorate reports to a senior manager (Assistant Deputy Minister) and is housed within the Strategic Policy and Research Branch.

Although all programs housed within the department are considered clients of the Evaluation Directorate, the specific users that participated in this study represented policy groups housed within larger program areas. Both of these groups use evaluation toward policy development as well as in reviewing program design and delivery.

Drivers for Evaluation

The mandatory requirement from TBS that all grants and contributions programs be evaluated on a cyclic basis, reinforced by the government's new Federal Accountability Act, is the core reason behind evaluation activities at HRSDC. TBS requires that an evaluation be conducted prior to a program's funding renewal and new program proposals must include expected results and key evaluation issues. Other mandatory requirements for performance measurement and reporting—for example, the annual Departmental Performance Report (DPR)—also draw on evaluation information to help populate department-wide performance reporting.

It should also be noted that other central agency requirements, imposed on all federal departments, help to ensure that the necessary infrastructure to do evaluation (i.e., resources for evaluation, requirements for formal evaluation plans, etc.) is in place. Additionally, the oversight role played by the Office of the Auditor General (OAG), in carrying out periodic audits of the government evaluation function and performance measurement and reporting, serves to reinforce compliance with government policies and standards related to evaluation and performance measurement.

The information needs of senior managers were also often cited by participants as a key driver of evaluation at HRSDC. In fact, participants referred to "a culture of evidence-based policy development" as a reason behind the demand for evaluative information. The Directors-General heading many HRSDC programs were thought to be interested in using evaluation findings and have thus increased the demand for evaluation studies. This is reflected in the large number of evaluations in HRSDC, some 60–65 ongoing studies at the time of the interviews.

Although evaluation is only one factor among many when decisions about programs are made, senior managers "do like to know what are the outcomes of programs, because it is a very large department." In particular, they are interested in the cross-cutting issues that apply to a number of programs and their policy implications. We noted that managers use evaluation information in program publications and other types of program literature. For example, a monitoring report published by one of HRSDC's major programs draws on evaluation information to help illustrate its effectiveness and impacts. Evaluation reports therefore constitute an important information source for those developing this publication, and serve to generate additional demand for evaluation data.

The Evaluation Directorate maintains close proximity to its stakeholders through a number of mechanisms. For example, the Director General sits on the Assistant Deputy Minister (ADM) Policy Committee, and there is a Departmental Evaluation Committee, chaired by the Deputy Minister, that provides oversight and guidance on the use of evaluation in HRSDC. This formal infrastructure provides a mechanism where departmental senior officials can provide the Evaluation Directorate with direction on the priorities for evaluation on an annual and multi-year basis. Traditionally, the Departmental Evaluation Committee also provides these senior officials with the opportunity to obtain feedback on completed evaluation reports and the management response that typically follows the tabling of an evaluation report.

NEW DIRECTIONS FOR EVALUATION • DOI: 10.1002/ev

Capacity to Do Evaluation

Although every evaluation conducted has its own unique context, a standardized approach to evaluation has been implemented within the Evaluation Directorate. A seven-step process has been put in place, from scoping an evaluation study to final approval of the evaluation report. In addition to these seven formal steps, evaluators can be involved earlier in the program implementation process; for example, evaluators are often sought out in the development of program performance measurement strategies.

The openness of the communications processes employed within the Evaluation Directorate, within specific evaluation teams and with evaluation clients, was emphasized by a number of participants. Directors report ongoing progress to the DG, who offers advice to the directors and their staff. Most of the directors reported using a collaborative management style in which the evaluation managers provide advice and make recommendations to them on particular studies. The evaluation managers also have access to external peer reviewers who provide input on the methodology to be used in a prospective study and on the findings obtained once an evaluation has been completed. The evaluation users also reported positive relationships with the evaluation teams, citing transparent communications as a key factor in their continued success. The use of evaluation advisory committees on all evaluation studies adds to this transparency since they generally include representation from key stakeholders.

The use of advisory committees serves as the key mechanism for involving stakeholders in particular evaluations. Members are typically asked to advise on program updates and to review evaluation reports. Evaluators usually have a positive view of stakeholder involvement in evaluation projects. One participant summarized the prevailing opinion of evaluators on this matter:

> . . . the evaluation is a lot more valuable if the organization as a whole believes in the results; and so if they're involved in the process of developing the evaluation, there's going to be a higher degree of buy-in.

One evaluator described the importance of involving program managers, in particular, in evaluation studies:

> They have their hands on information; they have more intuitive information about a program. So we need to work with them on that. . . . If we are in disagreement it is better to know early rather than later. The evaluation process is also a learning process for them too. Quite often things could come out during the evaluation. It may or may not be needed in the evaluation report but there will be things very important to the program. So they are always involved.

This last comment foreshadows an element of process use that will be elaborated below. Other stakeholders, such as program clients, other levels of government, and other federal departments are also involved in the evaluation process through, for example, discussions during the development of the program performance measurement strategy, or the preparation of the terms of reference for the evaluation to be conducted.

The conduct of evaluations at HRSDC is done using a blend of in-house staff and external consultants. Decisions on tasks allocated to contractors and tasks kept in-house are based on available resources and expertise. Internal evaluators are typically involved in developing a study's terms of reference, evaluation framework, and methodology. The field work is usually contracted out to consultants, using a variety of small and large contracts, depending on the nature of the evaluation work to be done. Even when evaluation work is contracted out, however, internal evaluators monitor the field work closely to ensure a high level of quality in the work produced by contractors.

On a more micro level, the evaluation advisory committees that are created at the outset of each evaluation study serve as an important mechanism to help ensure two-way communication between evaluators and their relevant stakeholders.

Both evaluators and users were unanimous in their affirmation that the HRSDC evaluation group is generally considered quite knowledgeable and that the evaluation studies that are conducted by this group are highly sophisticated. As mentioned by one evaluator interviewed, "The tools and methods we use are state-of-the-art for the practice of program evaluation and are intended to corroborate findings and produce defendable conclusions." Indeed, as mentioned previously, the Evaluation Services team has been formally recognized by TBS for the quality of its evaluation products.

The nature of some departmental programs and availability of rich databases allow for elaborate evaluation methods, such as econometric modeling. In order to conduct such complex studies, the recruitment of evaluators at HRSDC has focused on hiring highly educated, experienced individuals. As a result, 15% of the 55 evaluators currently employed at HRSDC have a PhD degree, and 60% have a master's degree. Particularly notable is that 45% of HRSDC evaluators have more than 10 years' evaluation experience, which is thought quite considerable in a profession experiencing heavy turnover rates.

Sources of Evaluation Knowledge and Skills

An important activity through which HRSDC has built its evaluation capacity is through the recruitment of qualified program evaluators. The department has participated in interdepartmental recruitment campaigns in an attempt to reach as many potential qualified candidates as possible and to reduce interdepartmental competition for the same evaluators. An attractive feature of HRSDC's human resource management practice is the Economist Development Program (EDP), designed to allow for entry-level evaluators to be assessed every six months against a pre-established competency profile. Individuals are able to continue this process until they reach an intermediate-level evaluator position. In addition to this, every effort is made to allow evaluators some flexibility in their role and in the type of activities that they undertake in their work. One such example is a regular attempt to let evaluators self-select the projects on which they will work.

A key activity in evaluation capacity building involves formal course-based training. At HRSDC, this includes both external courses such as the Canadian Evaluation Society's (CES) Essential Skills Series and internal activities such as specialized seminars on a topic of interest to staff. All staff members have learning plans that are reviewed annually, and each person may access up to $2,000 per year for training.

A variety of activities have also been undertaken in-house to promote capacity building within the Evaluation Directorate. For instance, evaluators are encouraged to accompany consultants in the field to get hands-on experience with various evaluation methodologies. Mentoring is a priority in the Directorate, and staff members are also encouraged to work in teams and share ideas with other evaluators. The use of consultants and peer reviewers has also helped develop the capacity of internal staff through their exposure to complex evaluative situations and discussions with experts. Of particular note are the "methodological conferences" that are held when a particular methodology appears controversial within the scope of a new project. Experts are invited to HRSDC to debate the merits of this methodology, and all evaluation staff members may attend the session. In addition to ensuring that the final decision is made using all possible information on the methodology, these conferences offer staff members the opportunity to learn about these methods from the very best in their fields.

Capacity to Use Evaluation

As noted above, evaluation serves a number of uses and users, some internal to the department and others more relevant to external audiences. Broadly speaking, evaluation findings are used to meet departmental accountability requirements (both internal and external) to inform policy and program development, to inform program managers, to provide decision-making information to central agencies in future funding decisions, and to report to stakeholder groups and the general public. In addition to these main uses, evaluators also work with program managers to assess and develop performance measures and identify "lessons learned" and best practices in policy and program development.

Internally, there recently has been a renewed interest in strengthening the link between evaluation and evidence-based findings to policy development: "There is a real appetite for this." Policy-related uses of evaluation can occur well after the completion of an evaluation. Policy makers use evaluation reports as a source of new ideas and to know what they should avoid in the future. Users of evaluation did stress, however, that evaluation is but one voice among many in the policy decision-making process and that sometimes other factors outweigh evaluation findings in these decisions.

It should be noted that a recent reorganization within the Evaluation Directorate itself aims at increased evaluation use. The creation of a unit involved in "feedback and knowledge management" is meant to generate thematic reviews and broad-based horizontal, strategic findings based on multiple evaluation reports, as well as following up on the implementation of Program Management Action Plans developed in response to evaluation studies.

Evaluation use is also a key concern for the evaluation advisory committees created at the outset of each new study. Such committees, through discussion of evaluation designs, plans, and findings, enhance connections and relationships between and among decision makers; they come to understand the evaluation process through their participation on these committees. The involvement of stakeholders is highly variable—stakeholders are free to choose how much or how little they want to participate in the process. This is often reflective of the importance of the evaluation being conducted or how much the findings are needed for decision making. Additionally, the senior departmental evaluation committee is very much concerned with the use of evaluation and the priorities that stem from reviewing evaluation findings.

Despite stakeholder involvement in planning, user groups sometimes believe that evaluators do not always fully understand the complexities associated with the design and delivery of large programs and so sometimes have the impression that the issues identified by evaluators are less than appropriate or not overly helpful in terms of generating information on the program.

Evaluations are typically conducted over a number of years in anticipation of program renewal, and findings usually support the status quo in terms of program design and delivery. Recommendations made by evaluators often involve relatively small changes to programs based on the more thorough understanding of a particular program's context or target audience brought to light by the evaluation. In most cases, evaluation findings are communicated to the evaluation advisory committee in advance of the publication of the final report, and so any changes required are made before the evaluation report is made final.

We learned from interviewees how evaluation has impacted program design and delivery strategies at HRSDC. For example, one evaluation found that the program under study had common objectives with a larger program and should be integrated into this larger program to produce more important impacts. The results of the evaluation were used to develop alternative design strategies and to merge the two programs together. Another example of design impact was an evaluation that found some irregularities within a program in terms of the proper implementation of eligibility criteria. These were remedied immediately and led to better targeting of program beneficiaries.

Participants also identified cases in which evaluation has little or no impact on program design or management. Such cases were typically due to methodological problems, absence of quality data, and issues related to the evaluators' working relationships with partners and clients.

Evaluation Enablers and Barriers

It appears as though evaluation is trusted in the organization and the opinions of evaluators are respected throughout the department. The department uses a standardized, "no-surprises" approach based on TBS guidance and professional standards for evaluators. However, in order for evaluation to become a part of the culture of the organization, evaluation activity should focus on the issues deemed most relevant by program and policy managers. This could be best accomplished, in the eyes of one participant, by putting an emphasis on understanding what are their needs and priorities and then responding to these adequately. Planning and communication then become critical components of evaluation and important responsibilities for evaluation leaders.

Key enablers of evaluation include the accountability requirements that are the main drivers for evaluation in the organization as well as the interest of senior managers in identifying the cross-cutting issues central to department-wide policy making. The organizational culture within HRSDC in general was also seen to be an important enabler for evaluation activities in the organization. For example, heavy reliance on evidence provided by evaluation studies allows managers to engage in the results-based decision making centrally required of them. It also provides managers with "a different look at programs and a way at getting constant improvement through policy change." Finally, and importantly, users felt that evaluation provided them with information that helped them learn how to improve the program, rather than simply justify its existence.

Another important enabler identified by participants is the approach taken by evaluators as they conduct their daily work. The extent to which they communicate successfully with evaluation stakeholders and their collaborative approach to evaluation were cited as particularly strong enablers. In the words of one participant, "the approach we take is to work in collaboration with the program as much as possible, so I think that helps them to see us as colleagues who will help them as opposed to people who will make your life difficult." It is important to note that many of the program community stakeholders at HRSDC have training backgrounds in economics and are therefore no strangers to systematic inquiry and evidence generation.

Due to high management support for evaluation, one participant felt that there were no barriers to the integration of evaluation into HRSDC'S organizational culture, but others identified the lack of timeliness of evaluation studies to be the most important barrier in terms of evaluation use. The process required to maintain a high level of quality often results in protracted timelines for evaluation studies (i.e., two or three years). One participant commented on the tension attributable to the tradeoff between rigor and timeliness: "…you have to get the evaluation done within the reasonable time, if it passes the timeline then it becomes just academic research."

Other barriers to evaluation use and to the development of an organizational evaluation culture include the retrospective nature of evaluative information and a lack of organizational understanding of evaluation. As one respondent put it, "some people believe in the program and don't think that outsiders can judge them; that evaluators can know the program well enough."

Concluding Comments

HRSDC, a service organization of the federal government, demonstrates exemplary evaluation capacity because of its investment in technical capacity and the rigor of its evaluation products. It has a large team of evaluators, divided up into a number of units organized according to specific types of expertise. Beyond the human resources aspect, it appears as though senior managers consider evaluation to be an increasingly important part of the decision-making process within the organization, and recent changes to the structure and positioning of the evaluation function point to an even greater role in policy making. In these ways, HRSDC clearly demonstrates strong "capacity to do" evaluation. The impacts of evaluation or "capacity to use" evaluation, however, are not always clear or well-articulated due to issues related to the timeliness of evaluation studies and the often retrospective nature of evaluation.

ISABELLE BOURGEOIS *is a professor of program evaluation at l'École nationale d'administration publique (National School of Public Administration), University of Québec, Gatineau, Québec.*

ROBERT E. LAHEY *is the president of REL Solutions Inc. and the founding head of the Canadian federal government's Centre of Excellence for Evaluation.*

Case 7: United Way of Greater Toronto (UWGT)

Jill Anne Chouinard, J. Bradley Cousins, Swee C. Goh

Introduction and Study Context

The UWGT was established in the late 1950s and is an incorporated, non-profit charity that is "dedicated to improving lives and strengthening neighborhoods" across a large urban district in Ontario. With more than 170 employees working in social research, public policy, capacity building, and other strategic initiatives, and tens of millions of dollars allocated per year to over 150 member agencies and 50 grant-funded agencies, the UWGT ranks among the largest of its kind in North America.

The UWGT is characterized by most participants as an organization in transition. To better align its organizational strategies in support of its priorities, the UWGT, along with other similar organizations across Canada, has been moving toward becoming a community impact organization, an organization that is committed to monitoring, measuring, and communicating the impact of its investments and activities. At the time of data collection, the UWGT was working in partnership with five other cities across Canada to identify what it means to be a community impact organization and to identify the tools and processes required to measure its impact. One of its key priorities, the Community Impact Measurement and Management Initiative (CIMM), was designed to build the capacity of UWGT partners to better identify and measure the impact they make. To that end, pilot projects in five different cities involving 17 different organizations were underway to develop a framework of common outcomes and indicators based on best practice research. As community impact is still a relatively new concept, some internal UWGT staff were not yet clear how this new emphasis would affect their work, though they acknowledge that much of the primary work that they do, such as their commitment to core funding for agencies, will not change.

As a large organization governed by a volunteer Board of Trustees, the decision-making process at the UWGT tends to be very structured and multilayered. Many participants noted that the organizational culture is changing and becoming more participatory, particularly as a result of new

---

We understand from our contacts at UWGT that the information provided in this case description is dated and that there have been significant developments over the past number of years, some that impinge on the organization's capacity for evaluation.

New Directions for Evaluation • DOI: 10.1002/ev

strategic initiatives, such as a neighborhood strategy, which now require more integration and cross-organizational functionality, bringing departments in closer communication and interaction.

Change in culture and organizational strategy, as well as changes in cross-organizational project work at the UWGT, also had an impact on communication processes, putting stress on coordination and integration across departments as well as externally with member agencies. Thus while communication processes are changing, participants did describe good information flows between managers and directors and between directors and vice presidents. However, some staff expressed that modest improvements in vertical information flows in communications with member agencies would be welcome.

Structurally, program evaluation has traditionally had no overt central function or unit at UWGT, but has been embedded within specific program initiatives. In the past, the norm has been to hire external consultants to evaluate specific strategic initiatives and address other evaluation needs. Again, this too is changing, as persons with internal evaluation responsibility had been hired over the past 1.5 years. With the move toward becoming a community impact organization, however, the approach to evaluation within all of the UWGT is changing. Evaluation capacity at the UWGT is thus conceptualized at two levels: at the level of the ECB services offered externally to member agencies and internally at the program level.

Drivers of Evaluation

Evaluation is becoming increasingly important at the UWGT. In the past, evaluation was externally focused, requiring member agencies to evaluate their programs and report on results. Evaluation is now becoming more internally focused, as UWGT looks at how it evaluates, why it evaluates, and what use is made of the information. This broadening of the lens provides some context to help explain the principal drivers for evaluation identified by participants at UWGT.

In 2003, organizational direction was established in a strategic plan identifying four priority areas: neighborhoods, youth, newcomers, and continuing to be a public voice for systemic policy issues (poverty, homelessness, domestic violence, and core funding). According to interviewees, the strategic plan has helped further define the way UWGT operates. Within this backdrop the transition to become a community impact organization is a principal driver of interest in evaluation and developing evaluation capacity at UWGT. The move toward a community impact focus is a pan-North American phenomenon, if not beyond, and as mentioned, is grounded in principles of evidence of results and transparency. Critical to this shift is organizational leadership which was identified by organization members as a driving force behind expectations for evaluation to become integrated in the internal business planning process at the organization.

For the UWGT, evaluation has always been part of a traditional accountability function tied to the principal functions of the organization. While donors have always had an interest in knowing how their contributions are being used, interest in program impact is on the upswing. As participants explained:

> We need to be able to say to our donors what's been the impact of spending your money. How has it made a difference either at the program level or whatever level? To be able to market that story, to help support the story. It is also important for agencies because how do they know they have made a difference?

> I think that we need to tell the story about impact to the donors. Donors want to become more involved. Donors are more interested, they're younger, they're coming from IT, they are a generation of people who want to give money, but they aren't just okay to give a cheque. They want to understand the story and they want to understand why they should give money.

This link to fundraising continues to be central to questions of accountability, and donors' increasing concerns about where their money is going and what impact it is having on the community.

Capacity to Do Evaluation

In the past, and not unlike many organizations in the not-for-profit sector, external evaluators were typically hired on a project-by-project basis, often only after the project had come to an end. A number of participants expressed concern that this practice did not address the issue of building internal capacity for evaluation within the organization. The recent hiring of three new, full-time people dedicated to evaluation-related activities signals a significant shift in the evaluation culture at the UWGT. Evaluators have been hired for a neighborhood strategy initiative, CIMM, and to build evaluation capacity internally and with member agencies. While all three internal evaluators reside within different parts of the organization and are dedicated to different projects, they are all involved to varying degrees with building internal evaluation capacity and capacity with member agencies and they coordinate through monthly meetings.

Many respondents indicated that there is no overarching evaluative framework governing evaluation and that the methodology is developed on a project-by-project basis. Methodology is often qualitative in nature and focuses on personal interviews with key informants, focus groups, and survey questionnaires. A number of participants also stated that they are very much concerned with building evaluation into the program planning process moving away from the historical practice of waiting until a project has come to an end.

Stakeholder involvement varies across projects and can be conceived of at the level of the member agency as well as internally. The UWGT requires member agencies to involve community members in a process around program planning and development and implementation and evaluation. According to one participant, they receive an "incredible range of responses" to a request as to how this is happening; working with agencies to develop buy-in around the notion of stakeholder participation was seen as important by some. At the internal level, there is often a team approach to evaluation when working on specific projects, and staff do try to involve stakeholders in the process, at least in an advisory capacity, right from the beginning.

Enhancing the capacity to do evaluation, particularly in terms of developing the knowledge and skills, is something that the UWGT was consciously working toward, the recent hiring of full-time evaluators being a good indicator. Although some participants defined their current level of knowledge and skills in evaluation as "limited," they are nonetheless keenly interested in becoming more knowledgeable and better versed in the area. As one interviewee explained:

> I know that I am interested in it, but I am also a little afraid of it, I have to admit. I've done a little evaluation. I guess it sometimes feels like an add-on and it would be interesting to figure out how to integrate it. How do you make it as part of the vernacular? What does it look like? How do you just do it so that it isn't so onerous? How do you keep it simple? And what do we do with the information once we have it?

Sources of Evaluation Knowledge

In the past, the UWGT has provided staff with some workshops and training. For example, in the last year they sponsored a workshop on logic models and on how to read evaluations effectively in order to understand what they mean. Despite these efforts, however, participants are generally self-taught when it comes to developing evaluation knowledge, as reflected in the following remark:

> There's a sort of interest and a willingness to try to access resources, books, etc., wherever possible. We have a library here, we have a clearinghouse as part of our website, our [director] will give us things specifically through internal mail ...

Other participants who come from member agencies have brought past evaluation knowledge and experience with them in their new positions. With the hiring of the new evaluators, however, sources of evaluation knowledge within the UWGT are changing, as there are now many more formal and informal opportunities for evaluation knowledge and skill development. There are more conversations about evaluation, more specific training around current evaluation topics, all of which is bringing a more consistent approach to evaluation and evaluative thinking within the UWGT.

As an organization working with member agencies, evaluation capacity building at the UWGT has primarily an external focus. According to one of the participants, "the UWGT is known for providing a lot of capacity building to agencies." In the early 2000s, the UWGT created a toolkit for organizational program effectiveness to help member agencies better understand how they work and how they might best measure the impact of their work. Along with the toolkit, the UWGT also provided a series of workshops to member agencies.

The UWGT occasionally sponsors workshops for member agencies and internal staff, sometimes bringing in renowned contributors. Most recently, the UWGT did a series of three workshops on the theory of change with a key thinker in this area. In the first workshop, all internal staff were invited to participate; in the second workshop, all of the agencies were invited; in the third, all pilot teams associated with the community monitoring and measurement initiative were invited. The idea was to provide a consistent approach and to get everyone on the same page.

Capacity to Use Evaluation

At the UWGT, evaluation results are used primarily as a "piece of information" for informing resource allocation and for program improvement. While evaluation results rarely, if ever, lead to funding cuts to member agencies, they can however lead to funding increases. According to some of the participants:

> So how do you integrate these learnings into the organizational culture. I think we haven't always done that. And then in terms of our funding, sometimes I think in an ad hoc way we look at how people are doing. We never de-fund. We might provide them with more support but we don't use it for decision making. It's a piece of information but it doesn't affect funding.

Evaluation findings do contribute to program improvement. According to one of the participants, a particular program initially had very negative evaluation findings, ultimately leading to its restructuring to a more effective entity. In terms of the use of evaluation results for program improvement and for decision-making purposes, however, a large multi-partner urban enterprise initiative was identified as an exception at the UWGT. It routinely used evaluation fairly extensively to help allocate resources, provide technical assistance grants, money for capital purchases, determine whether an enterprise is going along the right path, and to put in additional business supports, when required.

Within the broader UWGT, evaluation results are also used for communications purposes, to write descriptive "success" stories for future marketing and to provide program updates to the Board and to senior management. The broad responses provided to questions of use illustrate the evolving level of evaluation knowledge and skills internally, as well as the relationship between the UWGT and its member agencies, particularly given the fact that at the time the UWGT was not an outcome-based funder. The following remark illuminates how the organization grapples with questions of use:

> We don't internally see that information and say, "well that's a good job you did in involving community members, but this, on the other hand, wasn't. We really don't know how to use that information. We don't know what to do with it.

It was understood by staff and agencies alike that the UWGT will not de-fund agencies on the basis of performance outcome information, yet the UWGT does require this information in the name of building capacity to achieve outcomes. Despite clarity to some as to how and why outcome data are required, our discussions suggested that not everyone has the same understanding.

Evaluation is still very much in the initial stages of development within the UWGT. Thus while participants did agree that evaluation and evaluative thinking was not yet integrated into their everyday work, being involved and being around evaluation is helping to build a culture of collaboration within the workplace. As participants expressed:

> The value of just being in an environment where it's all still building and growing, even though it's not explicitly stated, means there's room for mistakes and growth on this journey right now because nobody really knows. There isn't anyone saying "well this is how we are doing this." These questions are still forming.

The community measurement pilot project provides a good example of process use in its initial stages. Relationships with internal staff and with external member agencies were helping to build knowledge and capacity around doing evaluation that were likely to exceed potential program outcomes: "This is not about the end product but about getting people interested and about building skills."

Evaluation Enablers and Barriers

We identified three principal and interrelated enablers of the integration of evaluation into the organizational culture. Leadership from senior management and from the Board of Trustees in terms of making a more formal commitment to becoming a learning organization, to learning from evaluation rather than merely seeing it as an accountability mechanism was mentioned by multiple participants. Second, participants talked about education and about developing a mindset around evaluation, developing an attitude and a willingness to learn and to change. The recent hiring of internal evaluators who will provide some focus on internal capacity building will help incorporate evaluative thinking in the organization.

Third, resources and time were mentioned as a means to helping UWGT develop a culture of evaluation where staff have the resources and can take the time required to figure out what evaluation means and how it works. According to one of the participants:

> I think people need to see the value of what it's going to be for them in their work. Why is this important? Is it relevant for me? Is it going to make my work better, easier, harder? That all happens through leadership. The message has to be this is why it's relevant and why it will make a difference to the agencies that you work with.

While the UWGT is making significant strides in developing an evaluative culture within its organization, participants nonetheless described a number of barriers to developing a culture of inquiry. One was the sheer size of the organization and the number of projects currently on the go. A related force was time constraints and the need to show results quickly in a very fast-paced environment, and within the context of emerging internal capacity. UWGT is a very dynamic organization with people engaged in all kinds of projects, making it difficult to bring all of the different pieces together, necessitating consistency, leadership, and buy-in. Building an organizational culture that values reflection and learning was viewed by some members as an essential focus. There are some signs that such a focus is beginning. We can see from the following quotation how evaluation and evidence factors in:

> The purpose of the evaluation was really to see where things could change, how better to allocate resources . . . it wasn't immediate, it took time, but the lessons were gradually incorporated into the way we work and as a result we started developing metrics against which we could measure success of the different enterprises. We've actually taken a much more strategic approach . . .

Concluding Comments

The UWGT is an organization that is in transition in terms of its evaluative capacity both internally and externally in its relationship with member agencies. While historically evaluations had been primarily conducted by external contractors, the recent hiring of three new, full-time evaluators who are involved in building evaluation capacity internally with UWGT staff and externally with member agencies signals a significant shift. At the same time, UWGT's strategic plan provides clear direction in four priority areas, along with clearly identified strategies for measuring process and outcomes for continuous improvement. The CIMM, moreover, not only provides for increased collaboration among all partners but provides greater focus in developing action plans and associated metrics to ensure that expected results are clear and aligned with input and output measures to inform progress. UWGT staff are very interested in learning more about evaluation and in building their capacity around evaluation, both internally and so that they can better support the needs and requirements of member agencies. While many staff were primarily self-directed and self-taught in terms of their evaluation knowledge, the community impact initiative is providing many more formal and informal opportunities for evaluation capacity building and training internally and with member agencies.

JILL ANNE CHOUINARD teaches organizational studies and program evaluation part-time at the University of Ottawa and practices evaluation in education, health, and community-based contexts.

J. BRADLEY COUSINS is a professor of educational evaluation at the Faculty of Education and Director of the Centre for Research on Educational and Community Services (CRECS), University of Ottawa.

SWEE C. GOH is a professor emeritus in organizational behavior at the Telfer School of Management, University of Ottawa, Canada.

Case 8: Ontario Trillium Foundation

Keiko Kuji-Shikatani, Catherine J. Elliott

Introduction and Study Context

The Ontario Trillium Foundation (OTF), one of Canada's leading grantmaking foundations, is part of a broader public sector, arms-length agency of the Ministry of Culture of the Government of Ontario. OTF's mission is "building healthy and vibrant communities throughout Ontario by strengthening the capacity of the voluntary sector through investments in community-based initiatives." Since 1999, the OTF has received $100 million annually through the province's charity casino initiative. OTF distributes 99% of these funds to charities and not-for-profits through two granting programs: Community (80% of disbursements) and Province-Wide (20% of disbursements). Within these programs, funding is allocated in four sectors: arts and culture, environment, sports and recreation, and human and social services. OTF receives 3,000 grant applications a year, and funds approximately half of these. The grants range from $2,000 single grants to $0.5 million multiple-year, province-wide operating grants. OTF employs about 100 staff of which two-thirds are located in Toronto. The remainder are located in 16 regional offices, with each office serving a catchment area for community granting programs. Learning to serve Ontarians better is at the core of OTF's culture. As one participant put it, "we have a commitment to having a learning culture, but also a service culture." Decision making is driven from the grass roots in response to local priorities and needs. Generally, interviewees felt that decision making related to OTF's core business operations is a group/collaborative process. Decisions can involve many layers of the organization in trying to "allow the final decision at the most appropriate level" but this can sometimes be time consuming.

The OTF manages its evaluation activities through a dedicated central function that also includes policy, research, and knowledge management (Policy, Research and Evaluation Unit, or PRE). Six full-time positions manage all of these activities. Evaluation activities comprise 20% of the PRE's annual allocations while the research component constitutes 25%–35%. The unit acts as an internal center of expertise that works with other departments such as Grant Operations, Communications, and Human Resources; PRE personnel also serve as evaluation managers for externally contracted studies. Other organizational groups also play a role in evaluation, such as grant monitoring and employee surveys.

In addition to the more common means of communications found in organizations, OTF has a well-defined schedule of regular meetings that provides a constant flow of communication throughout the organization. The regular nature of such communications allows PRE to maintain a close relationship with all OTF areas. This is very important since all are involved in some type of evaluative activities that would require PRE's expertise. PRE usually has their "finger on the pulse" of the foundation because of their central role: "Information at the board/strategic level is shared with us because it is part of our job to understand that." PRE also has weekly team meetings during which the director updates them on the latest activities of the senior management team. This information is necessary to direct research priorities and activities that will truly inform decision making.

Drivers for Evaluation

There are two main drivers of evaluation at OTF: demonstration of accountability and transparency and the desire to improve.

For OTF, accountability and transparency are "non-negotiable fundamental" drivers of evaluation as "an agency of the government that invests public funds." Accountability-related activities at the Foundation include grant monitoring, operations monitoring and evaluation, and the evaluation of the overall performance of funding.

OTF's desire to improve programs to better serve Ontarians was expressed unanimously by all the interviewees as a driver of evaluation. In order to achieve this, information gathered through evaluation feeds into the decision-making process at the senior level. Evaluation provides evidence to inform strategic direction and decision making at the board level. In the words of one interviewee:

> We have shown over the last few years that there is a lot of information that can be provided; and increasingly [the Board] depends on the caliber of information for the decision to be made. For them there is a comfort level in something that is based on fact . . .

All participants felt that evaluation is highly valued at OTF for its ability to provide information that can be used to improve programs. Evaluations are "very actively used" since staff realize that evaluation gives "them back important information." Evaluation is taken seriously by senior management and it frequently stimulates change. In addition, it is perceived as integral to accountability and is deeply rooted in OTF's learning culture. Here are some expressions of the foregoing:

> How evaluation fits is that it is very important for us to understand and appreciate the results and impact of grants—to learn from that and to continue to be more effective as a grantmaking organization and demonstrate to the funder that grants have an impact. Our core evaluation fits in that overall outlook.

...it really is about organizational learning. When we think about evaluation that is the context we think about it—as opposed to a more formal evaluative exercise.

Capacity to Do Evaluation

As mentioned above, evaluative inquiry is used for accountability purposes as well as program improvement at the OTF. Although all grants have a built-in evaluation requirement, the method/type of evaluation varies by the size of the grant (program monitoring for small grants, third-party evaluation for larger grants). Wherever possible, OTF attempts to reduce the bureaucratic burden placed on its grantees throughout the evaluation process.

The need to conduct externally conducted evaluations may arise in an "organic, informal" manner, coming from the Board or the community but the requirements are first discussed internally through prestudy consultations, based on existing data and information. Following the preconsultation, an internal reference group is involved in developing the Request for Proposals (RFP). Once a consultant's proposal is chosen, PRE together with the internal reference group will work with the consultant—for ongoing management, consultation, and subject matter expertise.

All those interviewed said that stakeholder involvement is "built into the process." The degree and type of involvement, however, depends upon the project. Stakeholders may be involved in reviewing the terms of reference, serve on the advisory committee, or participate in interviews or focus groups. They may also play a feedback role in the study or serve as a resource during research or prior to implementation. OTF staff is also involved as internal experts early on in evaluation studies as part of an internal advisory group. Stakeholder involvement is viewed as another "learning opportunity" for OTF.

All respondents indicated that PRE has extensive expertise in evaluation. PRE has consciously built an evaluation team with complementary skill sets. These are occasionally augmented when hiring new recruits by "looking for expertise not already evident in the unit"; alternatively, they build upon existing skills sets through PD and/or exposure to different types of evaluations or job assignments—working with more experienced staff in informal mentoring or coaching arrangements. On occasion, PRE will contract out for very specialized expertise or to augment its resources.

Outside PRE, the levels of evaluation knowledge, skills, and ability vary among other OTF staff; however, their collective contributions—through their different organizational roles—all serve to increase the organization's overall capacity to do evaluation. For example, management level staff provide the right environment and support for evaluation initiatives as they appreciate the value that evaluation brings to the organization. Many other OTF staff—who were former executive directors—have extensive community networks that can be leveraged for different aspects of evaluation (e.g., expertise and data sources). They are also supportive through their commitment to organizational learning and program improvement. In addition, there is solid evaluation expertise and experience on the Board, and there is an established feedback mechanism that allows results to be disseminated. Finally, there are many content experts who can serve as subject matter experts when conducting evaluative inquiry.

PRE explained that OTF's evaluation capacity has grown significantly over the last number of years. PRE staff indicated that they are at a "different point" now—they now have "a platform to do more capacity building and PD within the staff team . . . ." In the words of one participant:

> I know that from 2000–2005 we spent a lot of effort building infrastructure to be able to develop capacity to collect information from all our grantees [to make] sure that our reporting forms were asking the right questions, building a database to roll all that information out. I think we have reached a plateau that we now have a very robust data set that we can now more quickly develop a grantee report.

Another area of development mentioned by many interviewees was logic model development and use in the grant application process. The introduction of the logic model is helping OTF focus on outcomes and the impact of their grantmaking; and interestingly enough, OTF's capacity to use the logic model is also building the grantee's evaluation capacity. This is further nurtured on both sides through the Grant Operating Officers' coaching efforts—as they guide applicants through the grant proposal process. One participant elaborated:

> The huge capacity building piece that we've been doing for many years now is trying to educate the applicants about how to prepare their applications so that they use the logic model appropriately etc. People say that our application process is onerous, but they also praise it! It is very thorough—it forces you to focus, get all your ducks in a row and get your planning in place . . . they say that when they finish they are in much better shape than if they hadn't gone through the process. But they are so reluctant to put into place the targets. I am always coaching them on this!

In addition to periodic training sessions offered by external experts on a specific topic of interest, OTF also offers evaluation training through their biannual conference for their volunteers and staff. Also, "to maintain consistency in the grant operation," OTF conducts all staff meetings two to three times per year in which all OTF program managers come together to participate in "initiatives and projects." When probed, all the interviewees gave examples of OTF's "wide range of capacity building exercises" in evaluation. Essentially, capacity building is seen to be integral to their learning culture; and "highly functioning learners on staff are willing to try new things. [It] helps the organizational learning agenda."

Capacity to Use Evaluation

Over the last five to seven years, staff has increasingly witnessed changes brought about by a collaborative evaluation process and improved access to data (supported by policies and process improvement). This has fostered a "belief in evaluation" and an understanding that OTF can "make better decisions" that are evidence-based and supported by their "maturing capacity" to conduct research and evaluation.

Respondents felt that the majority of their evaluations have significant impact. They cited many examples of how evaluation has stimulated change—change in terms of process improvements, the establishment of new funding vehicles, identification of new granting priorities, and increased understanding of new sectors. These changes are largely reflective of the nature of the evaluations conducted—they were primarily needs assessments of specific sectors or targeted groups (e.g., recipients of small capital grants). However, there were other impacts articulated by the participants: as the internal "cycle of use" was engaged, all OTF employees have an opportunity to review the evaluation findings, consider the implications for their own regions, and provide feedback and healthy discussion about any issues, concerns, or questions they may have. This promotes learning throughout the organization as all employees are engaged in dialogue and contribute to continuous improvement and change.

OTF employees also indicated that some evaluation reports "sat on the shelf, had trouble getting legs," even after the "management response was developed [they were] slow in implementing." PRE learned from these experiences and developed processes that involve staff from the beginning of the process—to promote better understanding of the context of the study and ensure that there will be "actionable learning" that will lead to continuous program improvement.

All respondents talked about ways in which evaluation is used at OTF and how this has evolved in recent years. According to one interviewee:

> I think that is the big breakthrough in the past couple of years. I think we used to see the results as the *last step*, but now we see it as the *first step*. Now we receive the report and that is the trampoline that lifts us up towards action and concrete implementation. And so the final report from the consultants becomes the first step in the many steps that would happen internally to move us on.

Once the report is received, a deliberate cycle of utilizing the results begins. Through this process, evaluation results are translated into internal operational terms and used extensively to shape improvement. While the time to complete the "cycle of use" varies for each evaluation project, it can take up to one year for large evaluation studies. As emphasized by one participant, the objective is maximizing participation, involvement, and ownership:

> We have more or less formalized this new approach of involving people as much as possible, both in the research efforts itself as well as in the learning process and what comes at the other end. Because 'involvement breeds ownership' is what you ultimately want. You want people to take ownership for the findings and identify what they can take action on and do it. So it is a very, in a way pragmatic practical approach to how do we take the limited amount of resources we have to support evaluation type activities and maximize the organizational learning that comes out of that.

At OTF, interviewees indicated learning was an integral part of participation in the evaluation process. They felt that evaluation stimulates learning in a number of ways: by identifying previously uncovered issues during the process of evaluation, by giving participants important information about the program, and especially by teaching members through participation to become more evaluative. As one respondent explained:

> Involvement in the PE process has helped to increase corporate awareness of program areas; involvement in the process has helped to raise the awareness that OTF needs to be more expansive when undertaking evaluative inquiry.

Evaluation Enablers and Barriers

The learning culture at OTF surfaced as a principal enabling force for integrating evaluation into ongoing operations. In the words of one interviewee:

> Emphasis is on learning. And organizational learning changes the nature of the dialogue or discourse, around findings that flow from our research or evaluation efforts. People feel less like they are evaluated, in terms of their work, as opposed to invited to share in a learning process that can help advance the foundation's mission and advance work that we do—that is an important piece of it.

Although another enabling force is OTF's performance management system, it was strongly emphasized that people are the real reason that evaluation and learning have become part of the mental mindset: "the main driver is that people . . . really care about the organizations and their results. It is the old passion for the work." Staff engagement is further evidenced by the 100% participation rate in OTF's regularly conducted Employee Survey. Employees are truly interested in the future of the organization and how it can become even better than today.

OTF's organizational preparedness to benefit from evaluation is also an important enabler of nurturing a culture of evaluation. Since a period of substantial organizational growth beginning in 1999, evaluation has matured into a more participatory process that has facilitated its integration into the culture. As noted by a respondent:

> One of the things that is different that supports use is much more involvement broadly by the organization. So people who are going to use the information are very involved in the production of the information. And they are consulted and they help to analyze and they participate. So it is much more participatory. I think that is the main factor. People can see relevance to their own practice.

Finally, one of the most critical enablers of OTF's culture of inquiry is senior management's visible and ongoing commitment to evaluation. From the beginning, there have been "champions from the top." OTF leadership (CEO, funders, Board, and SMT) saw the true value in evaluation, became "active contributors to the work that goes on," encouraged and supported PRE, and nurtured the development of a culture of evaluation and learning.

Resource constraints—"cost" and the "volume of grantees"—were mentioned as the largest barriers by most interviewees. Ironically, it is the very success of the OTF that has generated the sheer volume of work to be done. This poses a significant challenge to OTF since they do not yet have the mechanisms to capture all of the data from grantees, manage them, and share them. For now, they focus on what is doable and perceived to be financially viable.

Resistance to change and time were also mentioned as barriers to evaluation (second in frequency after cost and volume of grantees). Other barriers reported by interviewees include: staff perception, resistance to change since "people want to stay the same"; "staying within parameters"; "grantees and staff being geographically dispersed"; "working with organizations with varying degrees of capacity"; "difficulty for volunteers to translate provincial findings into local context"; and the "long process of evaluation."

Concluding Comments

Over the last five to seven years, evaluation has become an essential component of OTF's overall strategy to promote organizational learning and knowledge management. Senior management has demonstrated ongoing commitment to evaluation and has supported evaluation capacity building efforts. PRE is viewed as an essential center of expertise; however, according to one participant, it would like to "become much more focused on the kinds of evaluation we want to do and where that fits strategically in the organization." PRE's ability to be proactive and flexible helped put the method into place that has made evaluation integral to the business of OTF.

Increasing OTF employees' awareness of the importance of evaluation is a deliberate effort as PRE intentionally tries to build a culture of evaluation through having more people involved so that everyone in the organization is more aware of what is going on around them, asking themselves the pertinent questions of what they are doing, why, and how to do it better. Building capacity in evaluation is OTF's commitment to organizational learning, based on the understanding that building evaluation components into every aspect of OTF's operational practice will garner information that contributes to their desire to learn and improve their services to Ontarians.

Notes

1. Available on request.
2. Available on request.
3. CEGEP is *Collège d'enseignement général et professionnel*, known officially in English as a "General and Vocational College."
4. In 2009, CBRPE was integrated with the University of Waterloo Population Health Research Group to become the Propel Centre for Population Health Impact.
5. Treasury Board Secretariat of Canada's program accountability mechanism.

References

Broadbent, E. (1999, February). *Building on strength: Improving governance and accountability in Canada's voluntary sector*. Final Report of the 'Panel on Accountability and Governance in the Voluntary Sector'.

Cousins, J. B., Elliott, C., Amo, C., Bourgeois, I., Chouinard, J., Goh, S., & Lahey, R. (2008). Organizational capacity to do and use evaluation: Results of a pan-Canadian survey of evaluators. *Revue Canadienne d'évaluation des Programmes, 23*(3), 1–35.

Cousins, J. B., Goh, S., & Clark, S. (2005). Data use leads to data valuing: Evaluative inquiry for school decision making. *Leadership and Policy in Schools, 4*, 155–176.

Labin, S. N., Duffy, J. L., Meyers, D. C., Wandersman, A., & Lesesne, C. A. (2012). A research synthesis of the evaluation capacity building literature. *American Journal of Evaluation, 33*(3), 307–338. doi:10.1177/1098214011434608

Larsen, D., Attkinson, C. C., Hargreaves, W. A., & Nguyen, T. D. (1979). Assessment of client/patient satisfaction: Development of a general scale. *Evaluation and Program Planning, 2*, 197–207.

Mayne, J., & Rist, R. (2006). Studies are not enough: The necessary transformation of evaluation. *The Canadian Journal of Program Evaluation, 21*(3), 93–120.

Miles, M. B., & Huberman, A. M. (1994). *Qualitative data analysis: An expanded sourcebook* (2nd ed.). Newbury Park, CA: Sage.

Nielsen, S. B., Lemire, S., & Skov, M. (2011). Measuring evaluation capacity—Results and implications of a Danish study. *American Journal of Evaluation, 32*(3), 324–344. doi:10.1177/1098214010396075

KEIKO KUJI-SHIKATANI is an education officer at the Ontario Ministry of Education in the Student Achievement Division's Research, Evaluation and Capacity Building Branch.

CATHERINE J. ELLIOTT is an assistant professor in the Telfer School of Management at the University of Ottawa.

Cousins, J. B., & Bourgeois, I. (2014). Cross-case analysis and implications for research, theory, and practice. In J. B. Cousins & I. Bourgeois (Eds.), *Organizational capacity to do and use evaluation. New Directions for Evaluation, 141,* 101–119.

3

Cross-Case Analysis and Implications for Research, Theory, and Practice

J. Bradley Cousins, Isabelle Bourgeois

Abstract

Chapter 2 of this volume provided a close look at the evaluation capacity of eight distinct organizations. The organizations were selected on the basis of their interest in and commitment to evaluation as leverage for program and organizational change. Having examined each of the organizations in terms of context, evaluation drivers, evaluation capacity to do and use evaluation, and forces and factors that affect such capacity, this chapter looks across them in order to learn more about the complexities of evaluation capacity. Beginning with a cross-case lens, we recapitulate what we found from the cases about organizational evaluation capacity and then present an emergent thematic analysis and discussion. The chapter ends with some implications for research, theory, and practice in the area. © Wiley Periodicals, Inc., and the American Evaluation Association.

We begin this final chapter of the volume with a reminder of a serious caveat. The eight organizations which graciously participated in our study did so about six years ago. The case profiles that form the basis for Chapter 2 within-case summaries were reviewed and

We are indebted to the following research team members for their comments, ideas, and insights on the cross-case analysis of the case organization findings: Courtney Amo, Tim Aubry, Jill A. Chouinard, Catherine Elliott, Anna Engman, Swee C. Goh, Keiko Kuji-Shikatani, Robert Lahey, and Steve Montague.

finalized in consultation with organization contact persons at that time. It is not until recently that we have engaged earnestly in cross-case analyses to identify learnings from the project. At the point of finalizing case profile reports, some organization contact persons cautioned that their organizations were dynamic entities undergoing structural and even cultural changes, some particularly in response to external environmental conditions and influences. There is little doubt that these organizations will look different today than they did in 2007 and this may be particularly the case with regard to organizational capacity for evaluation. We therefore beseech readers to bear in mind that the present analyses derive from cross-sectional research at a particular point in time and findings must be interpreted as such. Surely, a follow-up study to track organizational changes in their propensity to embrace evaluation would be invaluable to our understanding of the complex construct of evaluation capacity. But that study is beyond our present scope. What we can do is inform our understanding of organizational evaluation capacity in a way that has not been done to date. In this chapter, by looking across organizations, we describe variation in such capacity and identify the main factors and influences on it. Then, we present a thematic analysis and discussion of the principal findings of the research. Finally, we give some thought to implications for evaluation capacity building (ECB) theory and practice with particular attention to the role of empirical inquiry in bridging these levels of abstraction.

Cross-Case Summary of Findings

As revealed in Chapter 2 (see Table 2.1), our case organizations varied considerably. They were from a wide range of sectors (i.e., education and human resource development, community mental health and health, and societal and international development) and they represented different organization types (i.e., educational institutions, not-for-profit network agencies, charitable agencies and foundations, and Canadian federal government departments and agencies). Organizational size and scope varied enormously both in terms of annual expenditures ($15 million to $100 billion; $Mdn = \$145$ million) and number of employees (100 to 40,000; $Mdn = 900$). But the organizations also varied in their engagement with evaluation, the extent to which they had developed their capacity to do and use evaluation. Shared among these organizations was a common commitment or desire to improve the capacity to implement or engage with evaluation and to integrate it into the organizational culture.

Despite the aforementioned diversity, our overarching conceptual framework (see Chapter 1, Figure 1.1) fostered comparability and cross-case analyses. In Table 3.1, we focus on the principal responses to the research questions that we posed:

1. What is the nature of organizational capacity to *do* and *use* evaluation?

Table 3.1. Cross-Case Summary

	Case Organization[a]							
Focus for Inquiry	*(1) Dawson*	*(2) CMHA*	*(3) IDRC*	*(4) CCS*	*(5) CRA*	*(6) HRSDC*	*(7) UWGT*	*(8) Trillium*
Capacity to do evaluation	*Moderate*	*Low-Mod*	*High*	*Moderate*	*Low*	*High*	*Low-Mod*	*Moderate*
	Growing through conscious development, creation of policy and role.	Growing, resource constraints, limits on buy-in, university partnerships.	Capacity building, range of activity, attention to quality assurance.	Growing, tech expertise, external contracting, variety of evaluation activities.	Interest growing, high turnover, no external contracting.	Experienced, expert evaluation department, advisory committees, blend of internal and external, peer review.	New evaluation personnel, evaluation increasingly more proactive, commitment to ECB.	PRE[b] expertise, relation with community, program planning logic, content expertise, evaluation commitment.
Capacity to use evaluation	*Moderate*	*High-Mod*	*High*	*Moderate*	*Low*	*High-Mod*	*Low-Mod*	*Hi-Mod*
	Some history of use of findings, increasingly integrated through "ongoing evaluation," process use evident.	Commitment to evidence-based decision making, funding, learning, and accountability needs; some process use.	Commitment to evidence, reflection, and learning; regularized reporting; considerable process use.	Increased evidence-based discussions, performance management focus, results hierarchy, common evaluation language development.	Some recognition of recent work. Evaluation ritualistic, limits on relevance, need to "sell" value of evaluation.	Service to senior decision makers, thematic reviews, lessons learned, link to program design, manager involvement.	Resource allocation, use for program improvement and decision but project focus, some limited process use.	Increasing belief in evaluation and evidence, deciding grant priorities, improvements, cycle of use, staff learning, process use.

Continued

Table 3.1. Continued

Case Organization[a]

Focus for Inquiry	(1) Dawson	(2) CMHA	(3) IDRC	(4) CCS	(5) CRA	(6) HRSDC	(7) UWGT	(8) Trillium
	EEE-B	EEE-BB	EEEE-B	EEE-BB	E-BBB	EEE-B	EE-BB	EEE-BB
Principal forces and influences (E: Enablers; B: Barriers)	*Enablers:* senior commitment and championing, external support, organizational comparison, evaluation organization role. *Barriers:* some pushback and resistance.	*Enablers:* senior management commitment; experience with university on large-scale evaluation. *Barriers:* resource limits, dependence on universities, system constraints.	*Enablers:* commitment to use, use-focused approach, learning organization, research capacity. *Barriers:* financial partnerships, competing workload demands.	*Enablers:* relation with CBRPE[b], commitment to learning; merged inquiry traditions; results framework. *Barriers:* size, limits on time, resources, and buy-in.	*Enablers:* senior champion of evaluation; commitment to quality. *Barriers:* culture of audit, staff turnover and limited expertise, limited buy-in at senior level.	*Enablers:* accountability demands, adherence to standards, collaboration with program community. *Barriers:* timeliness, retrospective focus, limited buy-in in some quarters.	*Enablers:* leadership, growing interest in eval and evidence, resource availability. *Barriers:* size and organizational complexity; competing organizational demands, learning focus coming but not quite there.	*Enablers:* organization learning culture, staff engagement, senior management commitment. *Barriers:* resource constraints, volume of grantees, some pushback: time, geographical location, variable capacity.

[a](1) Dawson College; (2) Community Mental Health Association, Ottawa; (3) International Development Research Centre; (4) Canadian Cancer Society; (5) Canada Revenue Agency; (6) Human Resources and Skills Development Canada; (7) United Way of Greater Toronto; (8) Ontario Trillium Foundation.

[b]CBRPE: Centre for Behavioural Research and Program Evaluation; PRE: Policy, Research and Evaluation Unit.

2. What are the factors and conditions that influence the integration of evaluation into the organizational culture?

Capacity to Do Evaluation

All of the organizations in our sample were in a developmental mode with respect to their capacity to do evaluation but two organizations were particularly well developed in this way. IDRC and HRSDC, both under the umbrella of the Canadian federal government, were comparatively advanced in their propensity to generate evaluative evidence but through different means. IDRC, very much a learning organization and outside of the mainstream of centralized accountability demands of the Canadian federal system, routinely generated data for internal consideration and reflection through a combination of internal and external or contracted evaluative activities. Motivated by its obligation to meet central accountability demands, HRSDC showed great leadership in the federal community in producing high-quality evidence through evaluation, again through a mix of internal and external production options. It had received system-wide recognition for its contributions in this area. Both organizations were very much concerned about data quality assurance and had low tolerance for bad data.

Most organizations were on a developmental trajectory aligned with earlier stages of growth in evaluation capacity. CMHA, CRA, and UWGT were all committed to developing their internal capabilities for doing evaluation but they varied in terms of their reliance on internally versus externally generated evidence. CRA was striving to generate good quality evidence internally but faced some challenges, mostly aligned with the availability of knowledge and expertise, in doing so. CHMA and UWGT had taken deliberate steps to develop internal capacity to do evaluation, either through hiring personnel into newly created evaluation roles or concerted efforts to train staff in systematic inquiry. CMHA relied on partnerships with university faculty and staff as a mode of "learning by doing."

Through overt policy changes and commitments to developing the capacity to generate quality evidence for internal decision making and strategic purposes, Dawson, CCS, and Trillium were well on their way to enhanced capacity to do evaluation. Dawson relied on internal evaluative knowledge production spurred on by an overarching policy of "ongoing evaluation." ECB for staff was shaped by internal evaluation personnel in more or less of a coaching role. Trillium, on the other hand, had a well-developed and staffed evaluation unit and CCS had been instrumental in creating an external unit upon which it would rely to meet its evidence-based information needs. Both CCS and Trillium engaged in the development of overarching frameworks (results chain and cycle of use, respectively) for thinking about evidence and how it impacts on the organization's main business.

Capacity to Use Evaluation

Naturally, we observed a correlation between capacity to do and capacity to use evaluation but this was not stringently the case. Although growing in its capacity to do evaluation, CMHA appeared relatively well advanced in terms of the extent to which evidence informed decisions and met learning and accountability demands; they had developed some leadership within the region in this respect. Among all of our case organizations, we found varying levels of reliance on evaluation findings for decision making, performance management, and the extent to which evaluative evidence was taken seriously by senior management. Among those operating at higher levels of capacity to use evaluation data, the organization went well beyond meeting accountability needs to a focus on reflection, learning, and improvement. IDRC and Trillium were particularly well advanced in this respect, both having implemented structures to promote reflection on evidence (Annual Learning Forum, cycle of use, respectively). Likewise, HRSDC established a thematic review process that promoted the creation of knowledge across studies. Evaluation was seen in these organizations as holistic learning systems that rely on streams of evidence as opposed to a sequential production of individual studies.

Most of the organizations valued stakeholder involvement but some pushed very deliberately toward the involvement of internal staff in the production or review of evaluative knowledge. In this respect, process use was a cross-cutting dimension of organizational capacity to use evaluation. Dawson and CMHA deliberately attempted to infuse evidence production and consideration throughout the organization whereas HRSDC developed opportunities to engage senior decision makers directly in the development of meaning and understanding of data. With overarching systems and structures in place, CCS, IDRC, and Trillium all revealed considerable process use benefits including common language of inquiry development, conceptual clarity about organizational strategic direction, and sophisticated understanding of the power of evaluation to leverage change.

Principal Forces and Influences

Within the case studies, we gave considerable attention to both the drivers of evaluation (antecedent conditions and motivators) and the factors that affect the development of organizational capacity for evaluation. In many cases, these foci were inextricably linked. For example, HRSDC's commitment to meeting central accountability demands provided strong motivation for embracing evaluation as well as ongoing adherence to quality control mechanisms (respect of standards of practice, peer review). A significant cross-cutting force that fostered capacity development was senior-level commitment to evidence-based decision making and the role that evaluation can play in generating such evidence. In some cases, such commitment was closely associated with the top echelons of the organization, as was the case at Dawson where the CEO took deliberate steps to infuse evaluative thinking throughout the organization. Even for organizations that were more or less in the early stages of capacity development, such as CRA, the presence of a senior-level champion was seen to be a powerful force.

Organizational culture, particularly the extent to which there was a propensity to learn, was another factor that permeated many of the organizations in our sample. Such a culture was relatively highly developed at IDRC. A while earlier, senior management took a hard look at the evaluation studies it was producing and consciously recognized them as being inadequate to meeting their information needs, particularly their desire to learn. Structures were subsequently put in place to foster learning and an enhanced value-for-effort from evaluation. Other organizations aspired to be learning organizations and saw evaluation and monitoring systems as a way to help that process along. CCS and Trillium fell into this category. In some cases, reference was made to specific studies that served at some level as "wake-up calls" for the organization. Dawson and CCS both had experiences with the studies that translated into significant learning and motivating opportunities.

External forces and pressures were also somewhat enabling for some organizations. Alignment with broadly embraced community outcome initiatives within the not-for-profit sector helped shape UWGT's considerable investment in this direction. CMHA was motivated to show leadership within the region in order to raise its own profile and relationship building with universities helped them along this path. Similarly, Dawson was inspired by the knowledge that external regulatory bodies would be using evidence to compare it with other colleges in the system. Staff engagement with evaluation surfaced in several organizations as an enabling factor, one that relates in direct ways to the process use effects just discussed. This was particularly the case not only at Trillium, HRSDC, and IDRC as mentioned above but also at Dawson where all staff were exposed to the organizational initiative of "ongoing evaluation," and CMHA where staff routinely participated in the inquiry process at many levels from data collection to findings interpretation and reporting.

Our experience shed light on enabling forces more so than was the case for barriers to evaluation capacity development. Organizational culture was observed to play a somewhat limiting role with evaluation viewed by some members as an add-on activity that can detract from core business concerns. Limits on buy-in and ownership, at senior and lower levels, sometimes surfaced as barriers. Some barriers seemed to be organization-specific, such as the high turnover of staff with evaluation expertise (CRA), geographical constraints (Trillium), and financial relationships with external partners (IDRC). The relationship with the university sector not only served to enhance capacity development at CMHA but it also touched on a limiting influence. There was a sense that the organization was too dependent on university colleagues to go after resources for large-scale evaluations of its services.

The foregoing brief integration of findings from our collection of organizational case studies provides the foundation for the thematic discussion of the results to which we now turn.

Thematic Analysis and Discussion

Our cross-case analysis and synthesis has permitted us to identify and elaborate several themes of general interest in the consideration of organizational capacity for evaluation. Some of these emerged as we worked through the within-case reports, others through looking across cases. Ultimately, through the analysis of the principal findings included in each of the case reports and discussions and deliberations with research team members, we identified nine themes of interest. These we categorize into three higher order categories: organizational characteristics and dispositions, organizational evaluation strategies, and engagement with evaluation. The nine themes are summarized in Table 3.2. Each was observed in at least two but usually three or more organizations. We now turn to a discussion of each theme in terms of enabling and constraining considerations for organizational evaluation capacity.

Organizational Characteristics and Dispositions

We described several organizational characteristics in considering contexts for our case organizations (see Table 2.1, Chapter 2). Three such elements emerged as important considerations about organizational evaluation capacity. There were administrative commitment and senior-level leadership, organizational propensity to learn, and the nature of extant evaluation expertise within the organization.

Administrative Commitment and Leadership. Administrative commitment and leadership we observed as a cross-cutting and central force to the development of organizational capacity for evaluation. Often such leadership emerges in the form of champions for evaluation located in senior positions within the organization. Such individuals and administrative teams demonstrate commitment to evaluation through the development of organizational policies and procedures that rely on evaluation data. Leaders not only promote the use of evidence for decision making and learning but they also model it. Systems generating evidence that was ultimately not used were evaluated and reformed. Leaders were acutely aware of external accountability demands and how evaluation can play an important role in meeting such demands. Yet evaluation and evidence generation is seen as something much bigger. It provides mechanisms and opportunities through which the organization can learn.

Organizational Culture of Learning. Perhaps among the most salient cross-cutting organizational characteristic in our study was the learning function and evaluation's role as a learning system. Higher capacity

Table 3.2. Organization Evaluation Capacity Emergent Themes

Theme	Description	Examples (Case Organization ID)[a]
Organizational Characteristics and Dispositions		
Administrative commitment and leadership	Senior-level leadership and overt commitment to evaluation, championing, interest in continuous improvement.	Enabling: ongoing evaluation part of organization mission, strategic direction (1, 2); identifiable senior champion of evaluation (1, 5); adherence to external accountability demands (6, 7, 8). Constraining: general lack of appreciation at senior-level inhibitory (5).
Organizational culture of learning	Learning and reflection in high value, balance between accountability and learning, overt systems in place to promote learning.	Enabling: organizational learning culture (3, 8); commitment to evidence-based policy development (6).
Resident expertise	Nonevaluator organization members' expertise and familiarity with systematic inquiry.	Enabling: training in economics, social sciences (3, 6); interest in contributing to practical and academic knowledge base (4).
Organizational Strategies		
Organizational structures	Organizational structures and infrastructure.	Enabling: establishment of internal evaluation unit (3, 8); creation of opportunities for sharing and co-development (3, 7). Constraining: evaluation unit relationship with audit inhibitory (5); individuals with interest in ECB.
Partnering	Partnership with external agencies and organizations.	Enabling: direct relationship with external evaluation and research unit, university, agencies with research interests (2). Constraining: relationship with external donor partners with differing perspective (3), dependency on university partnership for inquiry funding (2).

Continued

Table 3.2. Continued

Theme	Description	Examples (Case Organization ID)[a]
Engagement With Evaluation		
Cycle of evaluation use and valuing	Successful use of evaluation leads to a cycle of increasing interest, frequency, and integration.	Enabling: experience landmark study (1, 7); multiple purposes and uses for evaluation (2, 3, 8); identification of cross-cutting issues for exploration/pursuit (3, 6, 8); participatory and stakeholder involvement focus leading to process use (3, 4, 6, 7, 8).
Direct ECB	Conscious and intentional support for ECB activities, resource provision.	Enabling: workshops and seminars with practice and academic leaders (2, 3, 7). Constraining: high staff turnover in evaluation unit requiring attention to basic skill development (5).
Evaluation tools and mechanisms	Development of organization-specific tools and frameworks to guide programing and evaluation approaches.	Enabling: results-based framework (4, 8); standardized approach to evaluation planning and implementation (1, 6); reporting mechanisms and expectations (3); centrally developed tools and resources (1).
External stakeholder involvement and relationship building	Involvement of internal and external stakeholder for interest identification, helping shape evaluations.	Enabling: community and program advisory committees (2, 3, 6, 7, 8).

[a](1) Dawson College; (2) Community Mental Health Association, Ottawa; (3) International Development Research Centre; (4) Canadian Cancer Society; (5) Canada Revenue Agency; (6) Human Resources and Skills Development Canada; (7) United Way of Greater Toronto; (8) Ontario Trillium Foundation.

organizations go well beyond meeting accountability demands and privilege opportunities to learn from data and evaluation processes. Organizational cultures of learning do not develop overnight; they are the product of myriad conditions and variables. Organizational learning can be triggered by environmental pressures at specific moments in an organization's history and conscious strategic decisions and directions. Evaluation has considerable potential as a learning system. It stimulates discussion and dialogue. It provides a basis for reflection on strategic direction not just in terms of what is working and what is not but what might be possible. In this sense evaluation is a means of both discovery and of challenging the status quo.

Resident Expertise. Although discernible through artifacts, policies, and procedures, an organization's culture is defined first and foremost by its people. We found evaluation capacity to be most well developed within organizations in which staff came with expertise that overlaps substantially with inquiry-oriented habits of mind (e.g., social sciences research methods and econometric analysis). In such contexts, familiarity with the power of evidence is high and evaluation represents one source of such evidence. Data quality assurance is held in high esteem and there exists a relatively low tolerance for poor quality. Staff are adept at conceptualizing and designing studies and are relatively sophisticated in reviewing and understanding complex analyses. In general, they have a greater appreciation of evidence as a basis for decision and policy making.

Related, we observed in some organizations a very strong commitment to advancing the field through systematic inquiry and research, for being recognized as a "cutting-edge" organization within the respective field of practice. While learning and accountability are universally recognized as fundamental functions of evaluation, knowledge production, in terms of contributions to the academic and professional knowledge base, is also seen as an important contribution that evaluation can make.

Organizational Evaluation Strategies

Organizational capacity to do and use evaluation is very much dependent on the actions that organizations take and the strategies they invoke. We found a variety of strategies employed by organizations to enhance the evaluation function and the extent to which organizations benefit from it. We categorized these under organizational structures and partnering.

Organizational Structures. Several organizations in our study had well-established evaluation units and structures in place and these were powerful in raising the profile of evaluation and the contribution that it can make. One organization (CCS) actually created an external evaluation and research center on which it would rely in order to meet its information needs. Depending on size, organizations sometimes are not well positioned to set up such units yet conscious efforts to invest in evaluation personnel and organizational positions with evaluation responsibility served organizations well. Dedicating staff and resources to the evaluation function naturally raise its profile within the organization, but perhaps more important to capacity building would be the internal relationship building that may happen. Evaluation units and personnel were seen to foster growth and development through resource provision in addition to expertise and advice. It is through ongoing relationship development that organization members, including senior staff, will develop an appreciation for what good quality evaluation looks like in practice and how it can be expected to serve the organization.

On the other hand, failure to build essential relationships may be detrimental. In the federal sector, for example, many evaluation units are organizationally integrated with the audit function. With a heavy focus on policy and procedural compliance and the independent assessment of such, audit can have a stifling effect on the real power of evaluation to leverage change.

Similarly, a heavy accountability focus, to the detriment of the conception of evaluation as an organizational learning system, may be destined to have effects that are equally intrusive. Since our study took place, the Canadian government approved and implemented a federal evaluation policy that prescribes ritual or punctual evaluations (100% of programs to be evaluated within a five-year cycle) and arm's length relationship between evaluators and program and policy decision makers.[1] Yet organizations in our sample that showed high capacity to do and use evaluation relied on needs-based evaluation planning and relationship building between evaluators and users. It remains to be seen what sorts of effects the federal policy will have on capacity development. Perhaps organizations such as HRSDC with a striking commitment to systemic learning from evaluation will somehow adapt to such policy demands while maintaining their commitment to evaluation as an organizational learning system. Organizations with less developed organizational evaluation capacities might be the subject of a different story line.

Partnering. For some organizations, particularly those in earlier stages of evaluation capacity development, partnering may provide a very sensible option to consider. We observed considerable process use effects across organizations in terms of their capacity to use evaluation. Such effects were usually the result of learning by doing. Individuals immersed in the challenges of mounting and implementing evaluations naturally learn and develop expertise and evaluation capacity. We discussed this as indirect ECB in Chapter 1 of this volume. The same may be said at the organizational level. The establishment of relationships with suitable external agencies, consulting firms, or university research programs has considerable potential to foster an organizational culture of learning by doing, just in the way that internal evaluation unit support and coaching roles can assist nonevaluator organization members to engage with evaluation and inquiry demands.

Partnering could have potential downsides, however. We have discussed CMHA's interest in developing its independence to compete for funding but how its reliance on university researchers may actually hamper that prospect. We talked also about the IDRC's challenge of financial partnerships with external agencies and how those may impact on the culture of evaluation within the organization. Yet, our sense is that partnering in the interest of good quality production of evidence is an organizational strategy with strong potential for developing internal organizational evaluation capacity.

Engagement With Evaluation

People and organizations do learn by doing and, regardless of whether partners are involved, history and experience with evaluation will sometimes help to leverage organizational capacity for evaluation. Four themes surfaced within this category: cycle of evaluation use and valuing, direct ECB, evaluation tools and mechanisms, and external stakeholder involvement in relationship building.

Cycle of Evaluation Use and Valuing. As mentioned in Chapter 1, in some of our prior research we identified a working hypothesis "data use leads to data valuing." This relationship is grounded in the principle that belief sometimes follows practice, which has been discussed and debated in the educational change literature. The idea is that it is not until persons actually experience firsthand the benefits of a new approach or way of doing things that they actually buy into it. In our study, organizational buy-in to evaluation as leverage for change was more likely in cases where there was a commitment to staff and senior decision maker involvement with evaluation (implementation, interpretation, etc.). We observed this phenomenon across a range of organizations. We have argued that process use is enhanced in such circumstances. But also enhanced are opportunities for organization members to experience the learning benefits of evaluation findings. In experiencing successful use or benefits of evaluation it would be natural that organization members would become more and more open to evaluation as a strategy for learning and organizational change. We envision this cycle of use and valuing to be somewhat of a spiral effect, particularly in the early stages of organizational evaluation capacity building.

Direct ECB. The themes that we present are interrelated, as can be seen in arguments we have made for learning by doing, process use, and a cycle of evaluation use and valuing. Such elements touch on indirect approaches to ECB but also important, we have learned, are conscious efforts to engage with direct ECB options and choices. Identified were training opportunities (e.g., graduate diplomas in program evaluation), internal workshops and professional development, and seminars featuring well-known contributors to evaluation theory and practice. The consequences of such activities are most certainly tied to direct benefits of evaluation skill and knowledge building and presumably opportunities for meaningful application but some may also provide indirect benefits such as stimulus for strategic discussion and debate, network connection making, and the like.

Depending on stage of evaluation capacity development, organizations may be better or less suited to some of these indirect benefits.

Evaluation Tools and Mechanisms. Integrating evaluation into organizational culture is idiosyncratic to organizational needs and exigencies. To that end, it is beneficial to develop or adapt tools to the particular context and information needs of the organization. The development of an overarching results chain or standardized approaches and tools for evaluation planning and implementation are likely to be more powerful and effective if tailored to the specific contexts within which they are to be used. Increasing familiarity of such tools would carry the potential to frame discussions and develop a common language of inquiry or even conceptions of the organization in terms of how and why it works the way it does.

External Stakeholder Involvement and Relationship Building. Described above are the virtues of relationship building to enhancing the organizational use of evaluation but most of what we discussed has to do with internal relationships between members of the evaluator and user communities. The preponderance of external advisory committees to help shape evaluation planning and design was evident in many of our case organizations. Sensitivity to the political, social, and economic contexts in which organization programs and policies operate is not only essential to the sustainability of such initiatives but also to the planning and design of their evaluation. In this way, the questions guiding evaluations will be more deeply grounded in a broad array of information needs including members of the program recipient community and, in that sense, will be more broadly useful.

The foregoing thematic discussion draws from the findings of our multiple case inquiry. We now turn to some final thoughts about the implications of our findings for ECB research, theory, and practice.

Implications for ECB Research, Theory, and Practice

We identified at the outset of this chapter, and indeed in the Editors' Notes for this volume, a serious caveat. The within-case analysis and reporting for the multiple organization case study were done several years ago (2007–2008) and despite our serious attention to integration and synthesis at the present time, these data are necessarily cross-sectional and time-bound. Yet they provide a close-up look at organizational capacity for evaluation across a range of organizations all committed to improving their capabilities in this respect. In this final chapter, we now stand off our findings and our thematic discussion to consider implications for moving forward. We do this by touching on three levels of abstraction: research, theory, and practice. Given the aforementioned caveat, we choose to begin with the first.

Research on Evaluation Capacity and Its Development

We generally see research as a bridge between theory and practice, a conduit between these two spheres of interest (Cousins, 2012). We observe that a preponderance of studies on ECB has been framed as reflective case narratives. These contributions are as insightful as they are lucid; they draw from personal reflection on practice and benefit from the practical wisdom of the author (generally evaluation practitioner). But as we have pointed out, research on evaluation in general, and ECB in particular, stands to benefit from more elaborate and sophisticated designs.

The present approach—a multiple case study of organizations relying on qualitative methods—has several strengths and virtues. The research is collaborative, the product of an interdisciplinary research team. It is guided by a conceptual framework informed by extant knowledge in the area and some original data. The study provided an opportunity for organization members, from a range of organizations, to share their thoughts and perspectives in their own voice. It also gave them an opportunity to review within-case findings and provide commentary and feedback. Given the range and caliber of organizations involved and the approach taken, we were able to look across cases in order to feed a thematic discussion. It is not our intention to generalize the findings but we do hope they contribute to ongoing inquiry in the area.

Weiss (1981) reminded us years ago that longitudinal designs are the preferred choice for inquiry into complex, dynamic social processes such as evaluation use. Carman and Fredericks (2010), in reference to their own research, concur that "cross-sectional nature of the study's design limits our ability to describe how the evaluation experiences of the nonprofit organizations might change and evolve over time" (p. 100). Just as organizations are dynamic and subject to rapid change and reform, their capacity for evaluation is likely to be equally as complex. Longitudinal designs, perhaps using mixed methods, would be invaluable in plotting the trajectory of change over time and exploring the forces underlying that change.

In the present case, we are not invested in generalizing our findings to other organizations and sectors, yet the question is of interest. We applaud the efforts of Nielsen, Lemire, and Skov (2011) and to other earlier contributors to measure evaluation capacity. Indeed some of our own research has been in a similar vein (Cousins et al., 2008). As Nielsen et al. remind us, quantitative methods allow us to move beyond analytic to statistical generalizability and provide a basis from which to assess organizational growth in evaluation capacity, comparing organizations, and the like. Yet the challenges of quantitatively capturing the complexity of evaluation capacity are formidable.

Another approach taken by Bourgeois and associates (Bourgeois & Cousins, 2013; Bourgeois, Toews, Whynot, & Lamarche, 2013) uses a mixed-method approach to measure organizational capacity to do and use evaluation. This work, which is grounded in the Canadian federal government context, holds much promise for intervention studies aimed at assessing the potency of ECB initiatives.

Theoretically Situating Organizational Evaluation Capacity

Our study elaborated on what evaluation capacity looks like in practice and what are the factors and conditions that influence it. Knowing what organizational evaluation capacity looks like is an important focus for research and conceptual understanding. Our particular approach explored the sometimes neglected aspect of organizational capacity to use evaluation and, along with Bourgeois and associates, adds to a more comprehensive understanding of the construct. The conceptual framework guiding our research was informed by different theoretical perspectives: organizational learning, ECB, and evaluation use. Based on our findings, we have elaborated and discussed a variety of themes that could be exploited to further understand what high-capacity organizations look like with regard to their interests in evaluation. Some of these are not new (e.g., leadership, culture of learning, and stakeholder involvement) whereas others provide fresh insights (e.g., partnering, resident expertise, cycle of evaluation use, and valuing). Further work on depicting and describing organizational evaluation capacity is needed and will help develop a deeper understanding of what good practice looks like than is presently the case.

But knowing what exemplary levels of capacity look like in practice does not necessarily imply that organizations will know how to get there. The study of organizational evaluation capacity is, in and of itself (and not unlike most other interests in organizational development), largely *a-theoretical* in this regard. We may learn a lot about organizations that are high functioning and high performing in their engagement with and use of evaluation. What is missing is a theory of change, a theoretical framework for organizational improvement in evaluation capacity. In this regard, the field is showing much promise.

First, recent studies and syntheses of literature have led to the development of conceptual models of ECB. The integrated model of Labin and associates (Labin, Duffy, Meyers, Wandersman, & Lesesne, 2012) and the multidisciplinary model of Preskill and Boyle (2008) are two that spring to mind. With an interest in developing organizational capacity, both models are theoretical in orientation. Labin and colleagues present a framework that is set up as a results chain. They integrate and summarize what is known about ECB needs, activities, and results and noted some "preliminary results of relationships between strategies and outcomes" (p. 329). Their study represents an excellent start on structuring the knowledge base and ongoing work on "articulating ECB processes" and more rigorous measures and evaluations of these processes will enhance theoretical understanding of ECB. Preskill and Boyle (2008) sought to develop an overarching conceptual model that describes how ECB should be designed and implemented to maximize its success. Their model offers theoretical propositions such as the following:

NEW DIRECTIONS FOR EVALUATION • DOI: 10.1002/ev

We propose that the extent to which and the ways in which the organization's *leadership* values learning and evaluation, creates a *culture* of inquiry, has the necessary *systems and structures* for engaging in evaluation practice, and provides *communication* channels and opportunities to access and disseminate evaluation information will significantly affect not only if and how people learn about evaluation but also the extent to which evaluation practice becomes sustained. (p. 445)

How can findings from the present inquiry add value? Our suggestion is that the present findings can help inform model development by elaborating the evaluation capacity construct. Despite some overt attention to the construct of organizational capacity to use evaluation, we believe the aforementioned models would benefit in expanding their treatment of this construct.

Second, the work of Bourgeois and associates (Bourgeois & Cousins, 2013; Bourgeois et al., 2013) proposes an evidence-based multidimensional profile of organizational capacity to do and use evaluation. This profile conception not only lays out what exemplary practice looks like (albeit in the federal government sector) but it also provides a growth scheme helping to understand what organizational movement from typical toward exemplary practice looks like. Such a scheme is suggested to be a valuable tool for organizational self-diagnosis and planning. But it can also be used in research on growth in evaluation capacity at the organizational level.

Finally, one of our own thematic discussions—cycle of evaluation use and valuing—moves beyond the a-theoretical description of good practice into the domain of organizational development and improvement. We are excited about this working hypothesis and consider it to be worthy of considerable attention for research on ECB. Through longitudinal and mixed-methods designs, we need to test this hypothesis and add to knowledge and understanding about how experience with evaluation, specifically the successful use of evaluation, can lead to growth in organizational capacity to do and use it.

Moving Practice Forward

We are somewhat reluctant to comment on implications for practice because our findings are not statistically generalizable, as Nielsen et al. (2011) put it, not to mention the foregoing discussion about ECB theory development. Yet our analysis and discussion do provide some lessons for consideration from a practical standpoint. We conclude this chapter with a list of issues for consideration for organizations interested in the prospect of developing their capacity to do and use evaluation:

- *Make evaluation visible.* Administrative commitment and leadership help organizations to develop their capacity for evaluation but the mechanisms through which this can happen are many and varied. Some suggestions include establishing organizational structures, policies and procedures, incentive mechanisms (awards and recognition), and the like

- *Foster successful use.* If belief does truly follow practice organization members need to experience the benefits of evaluation, either the use of findings or process use. Through a combination of pressure and support, ensure that the likelihood of such experiences will be forthcoming.
- *Derive indirect benefit from direct ECB.* Training and support will always be an integral part of ECB and the direct benefits are likely to be obvious. Yet it may be possible to get more mileage out of direct ECB initiatives. Integrate training with professional sharing, discussion, and debate. Use such opportunities to move beyond knowledge and skill development.
- *Capitalize on resident expertise.* Consider the range of expertise within the organization and which aspects are likely to overlap with evaluation interests, systematic inquiry, and the like. To the extent possible engage such members in evaluation activities.
- *Invoke partnering.* Particularly for smaller organizations with limited resources, there may be much to be gained in partnering with external agencies, organizations, or units. Learning by doing is a powerful approach to capacity development. Collaborating with like-minded partner organizations provides an option for learning by doing.
- *Promote internal coaching and mentoring.* It was not uncommon for us to observe an instructional or capacity building role for evaluation units and trained evaluation personnel working within the organization. Encouraging this sort of role would provide another route to learning by doing and it would enhance relationship building between evaluators and users within the organization, thereby enhancing the prospects for use.

Concluding Comment

Increasingly, it seems that organizations are being asked to do more with less. Evaluation can play a significant role in identifying areas of organizational and program practice that require attention or where changes, sometimes significant changes, may be warranted. Sound, credible evaluation will always provide decision makers with an effective way to meet accountability demands. But evaluation can provide much more as we have seen in a number of the organizations included in this study. Discovery about the functioning of organizational and program processes and procedures, new understandings about the complexities of internal and external contexts, and challenges to assumptions about how organizations and programs work are some of the "added-value" contributions that evaluation can make. We began with an elaborated view of organizational evaluation capacity that identifies the capacity to use evaluation as an essential dimension. The subsequent multiple case study added to our understanding about what such capacity looks like in practice and about sensible directions for ongoing inquiry. ECB continues to represent a fertile domain for inquiry in our field.

We end this chapter with a salute to the organizations that graciously agreed to participate in the study. Their openness and genuine interest in helping advance evaluation theory and practice through participation in the research was as commendable as their commitment to organizational improvement in the interest of long-term sustainability. This, we think many would agree, is a hallmark of strong and purposeful organizational leadership.

Note

1. http://www.tbs-sct.gc.ca/pol/doc-eng.aspx?id=15024

References

Bourgeois, I., & Cousins, J. B. (2013). Understanding dimensions of organizational evaluation capacity. *American Journal of Evaluation, 34*(3), 299–319.

Bourgeois, I., Toews, E., Whynot, J., & Lamarche, M. K. (2013). Measuring organizational evaluation capacity in the Canadian Federal Government. *Canadian Journal of Program Evaluation, 28*(2), 1–19.

Carman, J. G., & Fredericks, K. A. (2010). Evaluation capacity and nonprofit organizations: Is the glass half-empty or half-full? *American Journal of Evaluation, 31*(1), 81–104.

Cousins, J. B. (2012). Privileging empiricism in our profession: Understanding use through systematic inquiry. In M. C. Alkin (Ed.), *Evaluation roots* (2nd ed., pp. 344–352). Thousand Oaks, CA: Sage.

Cousins, J. B., Elliott, C., Amo, C., Bourgeois, I., Chouinard, J. A., Goh, S. C., & Lahey, R. (2008). Organizational capacity to do and use evaluation: Results of a pan-Canadian survey of evaluators. *Canadian Journal of Program Evaluation, 23*(3), 1–35.

Labin, S., Duffy, J. L., Meyers, D. C., Wandersman, A., & Lesesne, C. A. (2012). A research synthesis of the evaluation capacity building literature. *American Journal of Evaluation, 33*, 307–338.

Nielsen, S. B., Lemire, S., & Skov, M. (2011). Measuring evaluation capacity—Results and implications of a Danish study. *American Journal of Evaluation, 32*(3), 324–344.

Preskill, H., & Boyle, S. (2008). A multidisciplinary model of evaluation capacity building. *American Journal of Evaluation, 29*(4), 443–459.

Weiss, C. H. (1981). Measuring the use of evaluation. In J. A. Ciarlo (Ed.), *Utilizing evaluation: Concepts and measurement techniques* (pp. 17–33). Beverly Hills, CA: Sage.

J. BRADLEY COUSINS *is a professor of educational evaluation at the Faculty of Education and Director of the Centre for Research on Educational and Community Services (CRECS), University of Ottawa.*

ISABELLE BOURGEOIS *is a professor of program evaluation at l'École nationale d'administration publique (National School of Public Administration), University of Québec, Gatineau, Québec.*

Cousins, J. B., & Bourgeois, I. (2014). Postscript: That was then, this is now. In J. B. Cousins & I. Bourgeois (Eds.), *Organizational capacity to do and use evaluation. New Directions for Evaluation, 141*, 121–123.

4

Postscript: That Was Then, This Is Now

J. Bradley Cousins, Isabelle Bourgeois

Abstract

We provide some concluding reflections about the sustainability of organizational capacity for evaluation arising from informal communications with some of our case organizations. © Wiley Periodicals, Inc., and the American Evaluation Association.

As we have been clear about from the outset, data collection for this project took place in 2007 and final case profile reports for our participating organizations were signed off in 2007–2008. Our study is cross-sectional and dated. We provided a caveat in the Editors' Notes, we elaborate in the methods specifications (Chapters 2 and 3), and we came back to it in reflections on implications for ongoing research (Chapter 3). In short, we recognized full well that organizations and the contexts in which they exist are dynamic and ever-changing and it is entirely likely if not probable that organizations are in a different space with regard to evaluation capacity, learning capacity, culture, climate, and other significant attributes. This is all well and good, but the story does not end there.

As a professional courtesy we communicated with our case organizations prior to publication and advised them of our intent to publish and to frame the study as cross-sectional and dated. In two of the cases, the contact person at the time of the study was no longer with the organization and we exchanged with organization members we believed to be best positioned to hear from us on behalf of the organization. We shared the draft table of contents and streamlined presentation of their case profile. In some cases, we provided them with the draft editors' notes where we laid out the aforementioned caveat. This process was revealing to us in significant ways.

Through some informal exchanges it became clear to us that essential elements and aspects of organizational capacity and the systems that we described had changed, sometimes quite dramatically. One organization expressed enthusiasm at the prospect of a follow-up study to chronicle change in organizational evaluation capacity. Another requested that we include a footnote in their case profile stipulating that the organization has changed considerably since the case profile report was finalized. Another advised us that the evaluation and organizational systems that we described no longer exist. We cannot comment on the extent to which dramatic change was apparent across organizations or the reasons for such change; we simply do not have sufficient reliable evidence to support such comment and a focus on evolutionary patterns of this sort is well beyond the scope and interests of this volume. What we can do is comment on the fragility of organizational capacity to do and use evaluation and underline the warrant for ongoing longitudinal research on organizational change in evaluation capacity, positive and negative, and the forces and conditions that serve to bring it about.

There is a vast stream of inquiry about organizational change and the conditions and influences that shape it. This is an explicit strand of inquiry in organizational sciences and it is well integrated into applied fields such as education and health sciences. It is not, in our view, well integrated into the study of evaluation and particularly not with respect to the study of organizational capacity for evaluation.

Of course, all organizations must navigate ever-changing conditions and external pressures and forces. "Navigating the white waters of change" has become a popular metaphor among those interested in leadership and planned organizational change. Learning organizations have been characterized as being particularly adept at this through a variety of adaptive strategies, such as environmental scanning, capitalizing on triggering events, importing expertise and leadership, and so on. We have cast evaluation as an organizational learning system, a means to assist organizations and programs to leverage change.

Over time the field has come to recognize the primacy of context, systemic thinking, and complexity and their implications for doing and using evaluation. Patton's (2011) developmental evaluation approach is a leading example of a reasoned response to the problem of context and complexity. In his book, Patton provides a comprehensive treatment of the "adaptive cycle" of change and its implications for evaluation generally and developmental evaluation specifically. He points to the very real possibility that interventions and innovations may be the most vulnerable precisely at the time when they are at the peak of their performance. In his words,

Therein lies a potential rigidity trap, because context changes over space and time. Rigid adherence to a validated model … holds the seeds of its own destruction because things will inevitably change. (p. 208)

Can the same be said for organizations? Of their structures, their cultures, their value systems? And if so, what are the implications for organizational capacity to do and use evaluation? What role can evaluation play in helping organizations navigate the adaptive cycle and to change in ways that harmonize with changes in context and complexity? Our findings have helped us to understand at deeper levels than was previously the case organizational evaluation capacity and the factors and forces that shape it. Yet, particularly in the light of questions of longevity and sustainability, we have but scratched the surface. We have so much more to know.

Reference

Patton, M. Q. (2011). *Developmental evaluation: Applying complexity concepts to enhance innovation and use.* New York, NY: Guilford.

J. BRADLEY COUSINS *is a professor of educational evaluation at the Faculty of Education and Director of the Centre for Research on Educational and Community Services (CRECS), University of Ottawa.*

ISABELLE BOURGEOIS *is a professor of program evaluation at l'École nationale d'administration publique (National School of Public Administration), University of Québec, Gatineau, Québec.*

INDEX

A
Administrative commitment, 108
AEA Summer Institute, 9
Altschuld, J. W., 8
American Evaluation Association, 8
Amo, C., 9, 12, 17, 19–20, 26, 34, 51, 59, 101, 115
Attkinson, C. C., 63
Aubry, T., 9, 34, 43, 50, 101

B
Baizerman, M., 1, 9–11, 19
Barnette, J. J., 1
Birnie, S., 43, 50
Blashki, G., 12
Bourgeois, I., 3, 5, 7, 9, 17, 19–20, 23, 25, 76, 83, 101, 115–117, 119, 121, 123
Boyle, S., 10, 116
Broadbent, E., 60
Burgess, P., 12

C
Campbell, S., 60, 67
Canada Revenue Agency (CRA), 68–75; Agency Management Committee, 69; capacity to do evaluation, 70–72; capacity to use evaluation, 72–73; drivers for evaluation, 69–70; evaluation enablers and barriers, 73–74; Goods and Services Tax, 72; overview, 68–69; Program Evaluation Division, 70; sources of evaluation knowledge and skills at, 71–72
Canadian Cancer Society (CCS), 60–67; capacity to do evaluation, 62–63; capacity to use evaluation, 63–65; creating evaluative information, 65; drivers for evaluation at, 61–62; evaluation enablers and barriers, 66; Evaluation Studies Unit at, 61; Executive Leadership Team at, 60; facilitating evaluative activities, 64–65; facilitating evaluative learning, 65; overview, 60–61; Performance Management Team at, 60, 63–65
Canadian Evaluation Society (CES), 8, 71, 80
Canadian Journal of Program Evaluation, 19
Canadian Mental Health Association (CMHA), 43–50; capacity to do evaluation at, 44–46; capacity to use evaluation, 46–48; consumer needs assessment, 44; contribution to knowledge base, 44; drivers for evaluation at, 44; evaluation enablers and barriers at, 48–50; evaluation funding at, 43; evaluation knowledge at, 45–46; outcome assessment by, 44; overview, 43; program monitoring at, 44; public education and training, 44; securing resources by, 44; skill development, 45–46; value-driven agency at, 44

Capacity to do evaluation, 8, 9, 16, 105
Capacity to use evaluation, 17, 106
Case organizations, 27–28; characteristics of, 29–31; participants interviewed in, 33
Case profile report, 32
CBRPE. *See* Center for Behavioral Research and Program Evaluation (CBRPE)
CCS. *See* Canadian Cancer Society (CCS)
CEEC. *See* Commission d'évaluation de l'enseignement collégial du Québec (CEEC)
Center for Behavioral Research and Program Evaluation (CBRPE), 60–61, 62–63, 65, 66, 67
CES. *See* Canadian Evaluation Society (CES)
CES Essential Skills Series, 9, 80
Chouinard, J. A., 2, 9, 34, 84, 91, 101
CIMM. *See* Community Impact Measurement and Management Initiative (CIMM)
Clark, S., 2, 9, 11, 28
CMHA. *See* Canadian Mental Health Association (CMHA)
Coaching and mentoring, internal, 118
Commission d'évaluation de l'enseignement collégial du Québec (CEEC), 36, 38, 39, 40
Community Impact Measurement and Management Initiative (CIMM), 84, 86, 91
Compton, D., 1, 9, 10, 19
Consortium of Universities for Evaluation Education (CUEE), 9
Core Body of Knowledge (CBK) project, 8
Core competencies for evaluators, 8
Cotton, D., 7, 8
Cousins, J. B., 2, 3, 5, 7, 9–13, 15–20, 23, 25, 26, 28, 35, 42, 51, 59, 84, 91, 101, 114, 115, 117, 119, 121, 123
CUEE. *See* Consortium of Universities for Evaluation Education (CUEE)

D
Data collection, 28–34; case profile report, draft, 32; development (phase 1), 28–32; individual interviews, 32; report distribution, 32; review of documentation, 28–32; validation (phase 2), 32–34
Data use leads to data valuing hypothesis, 11–12, 113
Dawson College, 35–42; capacity to do evaluation at, 36–39; capacity to use evaluation at, 39–40; ECB model at, 38–39; evaluation barriers in, 41; evaluation enablers in, 40; institutional program evaluation policy of, 36, 37; internal professional evaluation unit at, 38; motivators for evaluation at, 36; sources of evaluation knowledge at, 37–39
Duffy, J. L., 2, 10, 26, 116

NEW DIRECTIONS FOR EVALUATION

ORDER FORM SUBSCRIPTION AND SINGLE ISSUES

DISCOUNTED BACK ISSUES:

Use this form to receive 20% off all back issues of *New Directions for Evaluation*.
All single issues priced at **$23.20** (normally $29.00)

TITLE	ISSUE NO.	ISBN

Call 888-378-2537 or see mailing instructions below. When calling, mention the promotional code JBNND to receive your discount. For a complete list of issues, please visit www.josseybass.com/go/ev

SUBSCRIPTIONS: (1 YEAR, 4 ISSUES)

☐ New Order ☐ Renewal

U.S.	☐ Individual: $89	☐ Institutional: $334
CANADA/MEXICO	☐ Individual: $89	☐ Institutional: $374
ALL OTHERS	☐ Individual: $113	☐ Institutional: $408

Call 888-378-2537 or see mailing and pricing instructions below.
Online subscriptions are available at www.onlinelibrary.wiley.com

ORDER TOTALS:

Issue / Subscription Amount: $ _____

Shipping Amount: $ _____
(for single issues only – subscription prices include shipping)

Total Amount: $ _____

SHIPPING CHARGES:	
First Item	$6.00
Each Add'l Item	$2.00

(No sales tax for U.S. subscriptions. Canadian residents, add GST for subscription orders. Individual rate subscriptions must be paid by personal check or credit card. Individual rate subscriptions may not be resold as library copies.)

BILLING & SHIPPING INFORMATION:

☐ **PAYMENT ENCLOSED:** *(U.S. check or money order only. All payments must be in U.S. dollars.)*

☐ **CREDIT CARD:** ☐ VISA ☐ MC ☐ AMEX

Card number _____Exp. Date_____

Card Holder Name_____Card Issue #_____

Signature _____Day Phone_____

☐ **BILL ME:** *(U.S. institutional orders only. Purchase order required.)*

Purchase order # _____
Federal Tax ID 13559302 • GST 89102-8052

Name_____

Address_____

Phone_____ E-mail_____

Copy or detach page and send to: **John Wiley & Sons, One Montgomery Street, Suite 1200, San Francisco, CA 94104-4594**

Order Form can also be faxed to: **888-481-2665**

PROMO JBNND